AF210114

The New System of
Global
Governance

The ongoing Paradigm Shift

by

Georg von Goldbach

This book is a revised version of
Part Three - Chapter 2 of the book

Europe on the Way to her Apocalypse
History – Background – Perspectives

Bibliographic information from the German
National Library:
The German National Library lists this
publication in the German National Bibliography;
detailed bibliographic data are available online at
https://dnb.de.
ISBN
Copyright (2024) Engelsdorfer Verlag Leipzig
All rights reserved by the author
Manufactured in Leipzig, Germany (EU)
www.engelsdorfer-verlag.de
Euro (Germany)

© 2024 Georg von Goldbach
Production and publishing:
BoD – Books on Demand, Norderstedt
ISBN: 9783759719751

Inhalt

PART ONE

THE END OF LINEAR SOLUTIONS IN GEOPOLITICS: THE OVERDUE PARADIGM SHIFT

"... how do I show the fly the way out of the fly-bottle?"

> Ludwig Wittgenstein, *Philosophical Investigations, §309*

THE SPIRITUAL FATHERS OF THIS BOOK

The intellectual authorship of this book is held by two American thinkers and visionaries. The two have never met in person, but what they have in common is that they derive their thinking from cybernetics as a scientific means to understand and explain this world[1]. This is obvious in the case of Gregory Bateson[2], because he speaks of it frequently in his writings. In the case of R. Buckminster Fuller[3], the reference to cybernetics is visible everywhere in his writings and also in his works, but he was

---

[1] Cybernetics is the science of controlling and regulating machines in analogy to the functioning of living organisms by means of feedback processes that receive impulses from the sense organs. In social organizations, feedback works through information, communication and participant observation. The science of cybernetics was born from the cooperation of scientists in the "Vienna Circle". It was formulated by Norbert Wiener after 1945, after his emigration to the USA, when he came to the realization that intelligent behavior can be described as the result of feedback mechanisms.

[2] In the case of Gregory Bateson, we are essentially referring to the collection of essays published as "Ecology of the Mind" in 1985. The English edition of "Steps to an Ecology of Mind, Collected Essays" dates from 1972.

[3] At Buckminster Fuller, our main source is his book "Critical Path", which was published in 1981. Probably his best-known book is "Operating Manual for Spaceship Earth", from 1969. It can be downloaded online from the Buckminster Fuller Institute website. The German edition of "Instruction Manual for the Spaceship Earth and Other Writings" dates from 2011.

more of a pragmatist and generalist nature. "Bucky" Fuller strove to live a life, in which he fought for the practical implementation of his ideas, mainly through the use and application of his design artefacts, while Gregory Bateson limited himself to theoretical and epistemological reflection and teaching.

What they both have in common is that they were very sharp observers of what was going on in the world and were always keen to understand how people acted. Both have always put people at the centre of their efforts and have always looked at people in a larger, more comprehensive context and from a system view. In Buckminster Fuller's case, it was "man in the universe." For Gregory Bateson, a trained anthropologist and biologist, it was the systemic relation between man and nature. What both have in common is that they saw the fundamental fallacy in human thought and action in the fact that man saw himself disconnected from these necessary systemic relations with nature and the universe. Both explained this as the result of the one-sided emphasis on the development of the natural sciences since the 17th century, which has led to a mechanistic world view. This paradigm of human isolation from nature and the universe, as both saw it, has slowly dissolved again since the early 20th century with quantum mechanics and new insights gained by biology in the self-regulating systems of life. These scientific discoveries generated progressively a new world view that related life and the role of humanity to the "uncertainty principle". A door into the unknown had opened. From now on, the meaning of life and human nature were perceived in a new light. It had become possible to reconnect with the nature of man and his importance in the cosmos.[4] This sums up the experience shared by Gregory Bateson and Buckminster Fuller.

In order to understand these two great minds, we would like to emphasize the decisive basic idea that is characteristic of each of them. Buckminster Fuller developed his fundamental ideas after 1930, formulated them in 1969 in his *Operating Manual for Spaceship Earth,* and summarized them with the formulation of *Synergetics* as *Explorations*

---

[4] Fritjof Capra gives a catchy account of this in his "Tao of Physics", of 1977.

into the Geometry of Thinking[5]. Intuitively, he seized the need for the application of "general principles and laws" to the understanding of the functioning of *Man in Universe*. He convincingly shows that it is not a lack of energy that inhibits the development of humanity. Rather, the fundamental mistake lies in the fact that humanity has not found, not understood, the access to the infinite source of energy that is provided to us from the universe through the sun. This lack of access to understanding eternally regenerating energy has so far kept people caught in a self-made trap. According to Buckminster Fuller, this phenomenon can be traced back to the work of British economist Thomas Robert Malthus, who established at the beginning of the 19th century the principle that humans would reproduce with the necessary fatefulness, but at the same time had only limited natural resources at their disposal. Hence, the fight for limited resources was inevitable. For Darwin, this became the struggle for existence and led Darwinists to formulate the principle of the

---

[5] This is the title of a book first published in 1975, in cooperation with E. J. Applewhite.

"survival of the fittest". If we take these thoughts just a few steps further, we end up directly at the rationale for the demand for "unlimited growth" of the economy, and at the political level, for the hegemonic striving and the seemingly inevitable wars as a means of gaining power, which are at the center of the critical analysis of our book.

Gregory Bateson is an anthropologist and a biologist by training. He has also worked successfully in psychology and psychiatry[6]. However, he has the most important significance as a researcher on epistemology, and in particular on the importance of cybernetics for the sciences and for the shaping of human living conditions on earth.

He says of himself that "the two most important historical events in my life were the Treaty of Versailles and the discovery of cybernetics".[7] This certainly sounds astonishing, because it is not immediately

---

[6] The term "double-bind", i.e. the relationship trap, was coined by him.

[7] In this part, we essentially refer to Gregory Bateson, "Ecology of the Mind, Part VI, Crises in the Ecology of the Mind, from Versailles to Cybernetics", from his lecture in 1966.

clear what the relationship between these two "events" looks like. We come closer to understanding what Gregory Bateson means when he says that, in his view, the "important question for history is: has the default[8] or attitude been changed?". He goes on to explain that "the most important points in history are... the historical moments... in which attitudes are changed", in which previous "values" change. He then shows that the Treaty of Versailles has not successfully changed the attitudes and values of the most important signatories of the treaty[9], i.e. Germany, France, Great Britain and the USA.[10] Therefore, according to his

---

[8] The term "specification" here refers to cybernetics, as a system theory, and means "leadership variable" or "decisive reference value" to which the other parameters and elements of a system are oriented.
[9] We should note here that since the October Revolution of 1917, a government had taken power in Russia with which the United States did not want to come to an understanding.
[10] As we will show later, it was precisely this thought that guided Rudolf Steiner in his assessment of the events surrounding the First World War. He insisted that it was necessary to change the political "rules" in order not to prepare a new catastrophe. As we know, Max von Baden, the last Reich Chancellor of the

understanding, the inevitable consequence of the Treaty of Versailles was the Second World War, with the same nations as important protagonists. He calls the Treaty of Versailles one of the "greatest relapses in the history of our civilization" and says that "we will have to deal with the aftermath of this betrayal for a number of generations to come", before adding that "betrayal in an armistice or in peace negotiations is worse than a stratagem in battle." His conclusion: "It goes on and on. The tragedy of fluctuating, self-propagating mistrust, hatred and destruction through generations".

Gregory Bateson is aware that cybernetics, i.e. "the second historical event" of his time, will not in itself bring the solution to our geopolitical problems. But he sees that it can be a contribution to changing attitudes and behavior. But he also knows that "any understanding can be used destructively". He summarizes his insight as follows: "In cybernetics itself there is integrity[11], which

---

German Empire, very soon ended Rudolf Steiner's advisory activities.

[11] Because cybernetics allows us to see the connections between events.

helps us not to be seduced by it into another madness, but we cannot trust that it will keep us from sin"[12] and then he adds in a more hopeful tone: "But this much is certain, that in cybernetics there is also the means to achieve a new and perhaps human worldview, a means to change our philosophy of power and a means to see our own stupidities in a larger perspective".

---

[12] We would like to note here that Buckminster Fuller also sees integrity as a very important criterion for good and successful action. That's how he called one of his books, "Ideas and Integrities", from 1963. He also emphasizes this point in his "Critical Path".

INTRODUCTION

The wider public has been talking about New Thinking for years. The media talk and write that we need "new minds". Even the "New Man" is called upon again and again. Others speak of the new "image of man.[13] To us, these wishes and demands seem to be fundamentally right and good, because we need new skills in the rapidly changing world and have to adapt our behavior to rapidly changing circumstances. But we also know that the New Man or Woman, or "right" and "different" thinking, cannot be prescribed. The physical man is constantly renewing himself, but a new spiritual man is formed either through spiritual revolutions, as in the Renaissance, or through experiences in lengthy learning and transformation processes. For the individual, this usually requires lifelong learning processes, spiritual renewals and personal transformations.

---

[13] In 1968, Arthur Koestler and J. R. Smythies published the volume "Revolutionization of the Sciences of Life, The New Image of Man", as a result of the Alpbach Symposium at that time.

So we have to ask ourselves how humans, we as humanity, can find our way to "new thinking" and to correspondingly new actions. - In today's specialist literature on this topic, it is often assumed that there is a difference, or contrast, between linear (convergent) and lateral (divergent) thinking[14]. Mostly, however, these remain philosophical or epistemological considerations pondered about at the academic level. The question of the conditions and prerequisites of how to get from a certain way of thinking, an intellectual or spiritual attitude, to a specific action is usually ignored. So the crucial question usually remains unmentioned, or is not dealt with in these discussions: how do I get from "right" thinking to "good" action? In the context of our topic, which is about geopolitics, this step, from theory to practice, is of course critical.

It is right here where the question of power comes into play. In politics, it is the question of power that must be put on the table, before changes and innovations may really be

---

[14] Psychologist J. P. Guilford introduced the terms "convergent thinking" and "divergent thinking" in 1956.

implemented, including the setting of "new rules". And then it gets very exciting again for any community of people and nations, and we are back in the middle of our challenge for "transformation" or change. The question of power is about: How do I deal with my own interests in relation to the interests of others?. Do I want to see the interests of others as equals? Or is it about setting the rules of the game in such a way that my own interests always have absolute priority or even exclusivity in a one-sided way, as in a zero-sum game.

In this essay, however, we will not enter into a discussion about theories and philosophies. We rather will explore the field of Global Governance to reach a deeper understanding of the future challenges the creation of a New System of Global Governance is facing. In this essay, we want to be careful and will avoid speaking of "right action" or "right system". For, a single human being cannot judge about issues of a global concern in an absolute way, as Immanuel Kant already showed in his treatises on the Categorical Imperative and Practical Reason. At the same time, we will not shy away from intellectual honesty and thus want to live up to what we consider our social and political responsibility. Therefore, we will represent our opinion clearly and openly, also bring examples and give indications of what we consider to be "better ways and more sensible actions".

We assume that a change in the way people think and act in our societies would lead to a social and political paradigm shift[15]. We consider this to be desirable and important in these times of rapid social change and communicative globalization.[16] We will

---

[15] The term paradigm shift was coined by Thomas S. Kuhn in 1962 and refers to "the change of fundamental framework conditions", whereby Kuhn in his work primarily refers to the scientific-theoretical and scientific-historical context by tracing and analyzing the process of change in fundamental framework conditions for individual scientific theories. In his book, he showed how paradigm shifts take place in the scientific field, what laws such a paradigm shift of rethinking and other actions follows. Since that time, the term has been used in many areas and can now be considered popular.

[16] Independent observers, such as the Club of Rome, Buckminster Fuller and Gregory Bateson, have been citing among the most important challenges facing humanity for decades: wars, management of natural

provide clear indications for the fact that geopolitics has been shaped for several centuries according to a pattern that is one-sidedly Western, and tends to be Anglo-American. Within the framework of this kind of geopolitics, the world no longer seems to be able to escape the rules set by the "West". It is for this very reason that a paradigm shift must be induced that allows the nations and peoples on earth to interact according to different rules, leading to a new balance. New thinking and acting are therefore important for all of us to escape the present plague that is leading humanity downward on a negative spiral[17] of violence and wars[18] in combination

---

resources, climate change, and rapid demographic growth.

[17] On the topic of the scope of action and the spirals of action, we also refer to the following source: Interview with Wolfgang Streeck from the Max Planck Institute for the Study of Societies about the scope of action of states.
https://www.mpg.de/6360276/handlungsspielraum_des_staates.

[18] In the tradition of modern psychoanalysis, Arno Gruen, for example, shows this need for action and shows ways out of this "psycho trap". Alienated from Life, 2019, Arno Grün. See also, Christoph Bördlcin, Introduction to Behavioral Analysis. 1st edition, 2015.

with an intensifying degradation of our living environment.

CALL FOR A SOCIAL AND POLITICAL PARADIGM SHIFT

In the following chapter, we intend to call for a paradigm shift in politics and the shaping of our societies[19]. Our primary aim is to show how attitudes, prejudices and ideologies hinder and prevent the redesign of social processes. At the same time, we want to show with a few illustrating examples how rules have been changed in social interaction and in politics, and have finally led to new and better results. Our governing power elites have brought us into difficult situations in several areas of life. We live in an age of

---

[19] The term paradigm shift was coined by Thomas S. Kuhn in 1962 and refers to "the change of fundamental framework conditions", whereby Kuhn in his work primarily refers to the scientific-theoretical and scientific-historical context by tracing and analyzing the process of change in fundamental framework conditions for individual scientific theories. In his book, he showed how paradigm shifts take place in the scientific field, what laws such a paradigm shift of rethinking and other actions follows. Since that time, the term has been used in many areas and can now be considered popular.

permanent and general crises[20], because these power elites pretend that their thoughts and actions are exclusively the right ones. Notwithstanding the situation, with an increasing number of crises, they do not change their minds to escape their ideological trap and still want us to follow their rules. We no longer agree with this, which is why we call here to openly question and redefine the currently applicable rules for the future shaping of our societies and for geopolitics, i.e. the way the nations are managing their relations on our earth. We will bring a few examples to show that paradigm shifts are feasible. Other ways, other paradigms of political action, and the shaping of social coexistence are possible.

We are aware that such a paradigm shift in social and political thought and action, as we are calling for, would lead to a social and political transformation with far-reaching social consequences, if implemented

---

[20] In a guest article for the Federal Association "Energy, Water, Life", Christian Schuldt, 2021, writes about the "age of crises". In an article in the FAZ of 15.05.2022, Philipp Krohn asks "Permanent turning points and new crises - how do we endure it?"

consistently, which would affect globally all areas of people's public and private lives.

Of course, we also know that change and transformation are always associated with new challenges and, most of the time, with risks. This is also the reason why people usually shy away from change. This fear of change is innate in us. [21] It is therefore only natural that significant social and political forces, as well as individuals, are afraid of a social and political paradigm shift[22] and want to prevent it as far as possible. Out of fear of change and the inherent risks, opportunities for social transformation are faded out and usually not seen, or suppressed and not

---

[21] In his studies, Konrad Lorenz has demonstrated in detail that "fear of change" is part of the basic equipment of the human psyche and human behavior. He was convinced that "for eons of time in natural history, those who were most afraid had the best chance of survival." On the subject of fear, see also Fritz Riemann: Basic Forms of Fear. A depth psychological study. 10th revised and extended edition (52nd–63rd thousand), Munich, Basel 1975.

[22] The Anglicism "paradigm shift" is also often used in German. We use paradigm shift and paradigm shift synonymously here.

seized.[23] As with all major changes, there are people and forces, who have an interest in maintaining the *status quo*, i.e. who will resist change. The reason for rejecting a paradigm shift is therefore a natural fear of change, or the fear of having to give up one's own interests and losing previous claims. This is completely normal and does not fundamentally call into question our intention or the importance of our examples.

As we have learned from psychology, fears and anxieties should not be suppressed, because, in one way or another, they will come to light in often destructive ways and often in the form of aggression. Fears and anxieties can be consciously overcome, and the energy that has been released by such consciously managed processes to combat anxieties and fears, may then be used sensibly for processes of change and

---

[23] In Germany, Karl Steinbuch published good and stimulating books on the subject decades ago. To start with, I would like to mention "Wrongly Programmed – On the Failure of Our Society in the Present and Before the Future, 1968.

creativity.[24] If we apply this consideration to the political sphere, then we would say that the energy and costs that we have been spending since many years on conflicts and wars could be used much better and more sensibly to improve people's living conditions. Hence, our proposal for a constructive paradigm shift, which would bring huge benefits to all of us, except for those who can see their salvation solely in the selfish pursuit of profit and the pursuit of hegemonic power.

By paradigm shift, we mean the change to a fundamentally new pattern of thought that will lead to a change in familiar reflexes and ways of acting. This will facilitate the taking of new paths based on new rules, leading to the peaceful transformation of social processes and of global political action. A paradigm shift is often compared to a quantum leap.[25] This points to the magnitude of the actual

---

[24] see h. Heinz W. Krohne: Psychologie der Angst. Kohlhammer, Stuttgart 2010.

[25] The physicist Prof. Dr. Markolf Niemz speaks of the meaningfulness and social necessity of a "spiritual quantum leap". https://spirit-online.de/ein-spiritueller-quantensprung.html.

challenge. A paradigm shift is not easy, but we will show that it is basically feasible.

We should also mention here that not every paradigm shift will automatically be meaningful and good in itself. One negative paradigm was certainly the globally widespread smoking of cigarettes that began to spread in the 19th and in particular, the 20th century. This paradigm prevailed, spread through intensive advertising[26], especially after the First World War. The American tobacco industry earned huge sums of money from this. At the same time, however, many people suffered considerable damage to their health. So, what applies for cybernetics and system thinking is also valid for a paradigm shift: without the right rules, a lot or everything will go wrong. As Gregory Bateson says: The rules have to change. And we would add: rules have to be changed in free and open debates among people, in *a competition for better ideas*, where it is not power and profit that are the decisive factors.

---

[26] Today, the "Marlboro Man" has almost completely disappeared from the public eye.

Every paradigm shift begins with first steps, which are often taken by individual personalities [27]who, in the face of a challenge, recognize the usefulness of alternative approaches[28]. Following such a first step of increasing awareness, an additional ingredient is required. It takes courage to

---

[27] The years-long struggle of European physicists over the understanding and interpretation of quantum mechanics and quantum theory, about the quantum leap in physics, is described very insightfully by Thomas Hürter in his book "The Age of Uncertainty", 2021. A paradigm shift is therefore not a matter of course. In the book by Thomas Kuhn mentioned above, the prerequisites for the success of such processes can be understood.

In the political sphere, we dare to mention Mahatma Gandhi here, who, through his courage, his personal example, but also through his perseverance, finally forced the British Empire to end the occupation of India. The "naked fakir," as Churchill called him, had managed to encourage the Indian people to shake off British rule.

[28] For an introduction to the question of social and political paradigm shift, we recommend the conversation, published in issue 16, Sozialimpulse 4/10, with Roland Benedikter, Stanford University. The questions were asked by Thomas Stöckli MA, Director of the Institute for Practice-Oriented Research Solothurn, Switzerland.

make conscious decisions. Finally, we have to recognize that only charismatic leadership can induce processes, i.e. lead people to consistently implement new knowledge gained to finally create new patterns of action. Such a decisive first step has been overdue for decades in politics in Europe and, from a global perspective, in particular for the USA[29].

---

[29] We will be told that European unification means a paradigm shift in German politics. We agree with this assertion insofar as we accept it for the policy of European integration with its so-called four 'freedoms', which concern the free movement of persons, goods, services and capital.

As we have been able to show in the previous chapters of this book, however, the paradigm shift that we demand for the fundamentally "better functioning" of our societies has not yet been seen and implemented by the EU. Freedom and sovereignty are indispensable prerequisites for the formulation of meaningful rules for shaping our societies. However, the EU, on the other hand, has become embroiled in wars and unprecedented dimensions of political and economic dependencies by subordinating it to the interests of the US and NATO.

THE END OF LINEAR SOLUTIONS IN POLITICS

Problems can never be solved with the same mindset that created them.

Albert Einstein

Crisis, or the chance for new happiness

As we will see later in this book, the industrial and social policy, which was characteristic of the industrialized countries in the last century, is built on fundamental fallacies that have consequently led to major mistakes and problems, for us in Europe, but directly or indirectly also for most other countries on earth.

We will show that it would be much better to meet the current geopolitical challenges with courage and intelligence in order to initiate a fundamental paradigm shift[30]. As the saying

---

[30] It is known, for example, that birth growth decreases at the moment when societies facilitate higher prosperity, better education and greater self-

goes: every crisis offers the chance for new happiness.

The following proposal is not revolutionary, so it does not call for an uprising or a general strike. Rather, it is intended to raise questions that, if answered, could lead to a process of social and political transformation[31] as a contribution to shaping a better future for all of us. In this sense, we are offering practical indications for creative solutions to global challenges, which will go far beyond the WEF's suggestion for the Great Reset[32]. Our creative solutions will be based on

---

determination for women. – But as long as the intellectual and material resources of humanity are used primarily for the production of weapons and for waging wars, these goals will not be achievable.

[31] To clarify the term, we would like to briefly note here that by "paradigm shift" we mean a fundamental change in a certain area of social life, whereby in connection with such a change new forms of thought, a new view of things and the world emerge. Transformation is a rather general concept of transformation, which is specifically formulated depending on the field, from mathematics to chemistry.

[32] https://de.wikipedia.org/wiki/The_Great_Reset

fundamentally changing the rules of the game.

After all, our call for a paradigm shift is not about "empirical" details. These serve us as illustrations. We call for a paradigm shift in geopolitics, i.e. for a fundamental change and adaption of new rules that enable and guide future social and political processes. The aim of a paradigm shift in geopolitics is to contribute to the well-being of all, and not only to increasing power and profits for the self-proclaimed elites.

Linear thinking in politics leads to a dead end[33]

The root cause, why we are currently experiencing this trend of ever-increasing crises and violent confrontations, lies in the fact that that most of us have so far only ever thought and acted in a linear way[34]. Everything should go on as before, only better, faster and further; always more, and more of the same. We were all told, drummed into us in schools and universities and reinforced by the media, that everything had

---

[33] That we do not get anywhere with such thinking, and how we can do it better, is very plausibly testified by Rene Egli in his book "The Lola Principle, The Perfection of the World", Editions d'Olt, 1994.

[34] In the book "The Discovery of Chaos", by John Briggs and F. David Peat, 1997; the original was published in New York in 1989 under the title "Turbulent Mirror", the authors convincingly and consistently show that the world of people cannot be grasped and understood with linear concepts. Nevertheless, these linear concepts still control the common narratives in politics today. Probably the best example of this is the publication of studies such as those periodically published by the Bertelsmann Foundation for the Control of Public Opinion.

to go on as before, only better; that is, faster, farther and more of the same.

This linear thinking is also the reason, why there has not yet been a paradigm shift in geopolitics. So far, no one in the "Western" countries has come up with the idea of a fundamental paradigm shift with regard to the actual challenges in geopolitics. Nobody in the "West" has said so far: let's try it in a completely different way, not linearly on the path we have taken of the past 600 centuries. At the end, we will have to acknowledge that the time has come to meet the challenging crises with a new attitude, a new way of thinking. Only a fundamental change will lead to sustainable solutions to the problems and induce a fruitful transformation of our societies, enabling a higher quality of life to be shared by all people on this earth.

In the following, we want to explain in some more detail what exactly we mean by this paradigm shift and how it can be justified[35] and what the necessary prerequisites are.[36]

An important premise, to which Buckminster Fuller in particular points out, has been known since classical philosophy. He clearly distinguishes between the function of the "brain" and the potentials of "mind". While it is the task of the intellect to serve us in the description of "facts", it is given to the mind to discover the *universal principles and laws* in order to understand and align with the synergies, which are providing orientation to our lifeworld and the processes that are governing our lives. If we engage in such mind-based thinking, we will become aware that we are advancing into new dimensions, which can open paths for new thinking and new attitudes towards a paradigm shift.

---

[35] We refer to Richard J. Bernstein: Beyond objectivism and relativism: Science, Hermeneutics, and Praxis, University of Pennsylvania Press, 1983.

[36] R. Buckminster Fuller in his "Critical Path", Foreword, page XI, but also on page 159, where he writes: "brain deals with... thingness" and on page 160 "only minds have the capability to discover principles". It is these "principles" that we call the "general rules" here in the sense of cybernetics.

In order to find the courage to think and act in new ways, however, we would like to provide at least a few examples of successful paradigm shifts to show that social paradigm shifts are feasible on a large scale and can make absolute sense.

SUCCESSFUL EXAMPLES OF PARADIGM SHIFTS IN INTERNATIONAL POLITICS

Even in the Federal Republic of Germany, which certainly cannot be regarded as a state with great revolutionary energy, there have already been paradigm shifts in certain areas. We would like to briefly mention just two examples here in order to show that even in Germany it is principally possible to fundamentally change the usual political and public action, i.e. not only to react on the symptoms in order to then create new problems, but to actually take new paths that initiate long-term, positive changes.

The policy of reconciliation and peace under Willy Brandt

Another example of a successful paradigm shift in the politics of the Federal Republic of Germany can be found in the reconciliation and peace policy of the government under Willy Brandt. Today we can no longer imagine how a large part of the population, instigated by political parties, resisted this policy of reconciliation with our eastern neighbors.

With his charisma and the support of courageous and clever politicians such as Egon Bahr and Hans-Dietrich Genscher, Chancellor Willy Brandt succeeded in implementing this policy. As a result, this policy has led, among other things, to Germany becoming a respected partner of our eastern neighbors, but also in global politics as a whole. The earlier trauma of the Nazi-era political past has since become a manageable part of our foreign policy agenda, and the way Germany has dealt with its great historical legacies in a courageous and responsible way has since become a widely recognized part of its political profile.

Through this paradigm shift and this courageous step on the path to reconciliation and international understanding, Germany has freed itself from the corset of the past. This also opened the door to the possibility of sovereign management of German foreign policy with regard to its Eastern European neighbors, but also in Europe as a whole, as a policy of good neighborhood.

There are also good examples of successful paradigm shifts at the level of international politics, of which we will briefly mention at least three to illustrate what we want to put forward here in our book.

Singapore: from Third to First World

In the modern history of the development of modern Asian states, the state of Singapore certainly stands[37] out as a very special phenomenon, as the result of a unique experiment that was not given much of a future, when it was founded. Today, Singapore has become a model state in many respects, which unfortunately has not yet found any successful imitators due to its uniqueness.[38] It is certainly not out of place to

---

[37] There is a very extensive literature on Singapore, covering all areas of science and modern life. As an introduction to the topic, we still consider the biography of the founder, Lee Kuam Yew, to be very helpful, "From Third World to First".

[38] We know that there are vehement critics of Singapore as an "authoritarian regime", especially in Germany. If we consider how many "failed states" there are now on our globe, and how many states are responsible for wars, and how many states do not succeed in offering their populations good health and education systems, or even in feeding them well, then

call Singapore a pearl, not only among the Asian states, but among the states of the international community. In Singapore, an exceptionally high quality of life has been achieved for all citizens on an unprecedented scale, and at the same time, it goes hand in hand with a universal realization of human rights.

Perestroika and German reunification

Another example of a successful paradigm shift comes from our European policy. We would like to refer here to the policy of *glasnost* and *perestroika* from 1989 to 1991 under the leadership of Mikhail Gorbachev, as it brought a non-violent end to the Soviet Union and facilitated the process of peaceful and non-violent German reunification. The Soviet Union's policy had reached an impasse. What would have been possible options? To detonate atomic bombs against enemies? To start a new world war? – Gorbachev chose a different path, he made a paradigm shift and

---

we think it is better to be a little "authoritarian" than "failed" or "problematic" in development.

banned violence and war from European politics, at least for a few years.[39]

Gorbachev relied on his political genius and took a different, non-linear path, taking a step in a direction that no one had seen before. He has extended his hand to the West in a friendly manner to usher in a new era by acknowledging the economic and political defeat of the Soviet Union. At the same time, however, he was concerned with proposing, on the basis of the given situation, a solution that would serve the long-term interests of the peoples of the Soviet Union, of which he was president, but also of the other European peoples.

This example makes it very clear that there was not only a linear "business as usual" in Gorbachev's thinking, but that he saw the possibility of changing the global political configuration in the world. Mind you, to

---

[39] In an interview, Richard Sakwa explains the basics: "We are at the funeral of the old school of diplomacy", published in Global Bridge on May 21, 2024. To deepen the insights, we recommend reading his books, such as "The Lost Peace: How the West Failed to Prevent a Second Cold War", from 2023.

change the world, and to do so without taking up arms. What a noble policy!

China's economic and social transformation

The third example from international politics that we would like to refer to briefly here is the change in the economic policy paradigm in China under Deng Xiaoping, the leader of the Communist Party and leader of China from 1979 to 1997. As an old comrade to and successor to Mao Zedong, he had taken on the role of the "outstanding leader", at the same time, he initiated a fundamental change in Chinese politics, especially economic policy.

In his position, he could not say, we are now abolishing the Communist Party, or we are turning China upside down as a whole. He was well aware that, after many decades of uprisings and wars during the first half of the 20th century, the country had to find itself and come into a rhythm to function stably and reliably according to new rules. With his open mind, he learned and understood during his visit to the newly industrializing center in

Southern China and to Singapore[40], that there must be an alternative, another way to lead China out of poverty and backwardness. He opened with his policies the way to this path and implemented it with a lot of political skill, which basically ended the previous paradigm of the communist mode of production and its centralist administration in China, the legacy from the time of Mao.

Since then, China has taken this new path very successfully.[41] Deng Xiaoping, in his intelligent and pragmatic way, asked: Where do we stand? Where can we go? What do we have to do to achieve this? What are our resources and opportunities? And it seems as if he has asked himself another question: which path can fit in with our millennia-old

---

[40] The relevant information can be found in the book "From Third World to First", by Lee Kuam Yew, the founder and long-time president of Singapore.

[41] We should remember at this point that China had successfully initiated its political transformation at the time of Mao Zedong, after unspeakable sacrifices, especially under the "Cultural Revolution". Economically, however, neither "the great leap" of industrialization had been achieved, nor had the rampant poverty of a large part of the population been overcome.

culture and tradition? – Together with the people who worked with him, he found the answer to this in the fruitful combination of the ethical rules and virtues from the tradition of Confucianism with the drive for personal success of the Chinese people. This complementary approach still governs life in Singapore today, as well as in modern-day China.

Based on the given situation, he understood that China had to fundamentally change the rules of the game for its economy. Free enterprise, within certain limits and in compliance with certain rules, was made possible and encouraged. At the same time, of course, this also brought great progress in the sense of individual development for people. Mao's strict and rigid, monolithic system had been broken up. There is a very telling saying by Deng Xiaoping in which he asked: "Which is better, a black cat or a white cat?" He gave the following answer: "The main thing is that the cat catches mice". Please bear in mind that this paradigm shift led to the creation of modern China. It was not limited to economic growth. Can we call that a successful approach to the "pursuit of happiness"?

This example of China explains the principle of a paradigm shift very well. It's not about choosing between black and white. Above all, it's not about doing more of what hasn't worked well before. So it's not about mixing black and white to give birth to a gray cat. No, it's about walking down a path that no one has seen before. Using China as an example, this new path for China, starting from the Confucian tradition, meant trusting in the genius and creativity of the Chinese people within the framework of the order set by the Communist Party.

From what we can observe, this paradigm shift in China is showing excellent results, unique in the history of mankind, in that a people, trusting in their own forces, develop in a way that provokes our amazement and admiration.

CHANGING THE PERSPECTIVE LEADS TO FINDING A NEW PATH

A paradigm shift in politics is not "witchcraft" and nothing that would be beyond our reach. It seems, as if we have been told for decades to always look in one specific direction only, because that is where the solution was supposedly to be found. This one-sided world view has limited our opportunities and led us to a dead end. We understand today that we have been led in the wrong direction, which has brought us into ever-increasing problems, creating crises and finally an impasse, of which we do not easily find a way out. Certainly, a paradigm shift does not fail due to a lack of knowledge, but rather because we fear change, and lack experience in taking new paths. We know well that it is often difficult for people to take paths that they do not yet know "from experience". The main obstacle, however, is probably fear, and the subsequent lack of will and courage to initiate and allow major social changes. [42]

---

[42] Horst-Eberhard Richter, the "grand old man" of the German peace movement, has dealt with this topic a lot. One of his books on this subject is "Morality in

So it is time for us now to change the perspective and direction of our thinking, to accept the challenge that is in our immediate reach. We need to steer the development of our societies in a direction that takes us away from the current problems, [43] rather than just managing them and replacing them with newly created problems.

Times of Crisis", Suhrkamp Verlag, original edition, 2010.

[43] We borrow this concept from cybernetics, as it was initiated in 1948 by Norbert Wiener together with other colleagues as a science. at the same time, however, we also refer to his socially critical, popular scientific work "The Human Use of Human Beings – Cybernetics and Society", in which he refers to the necessity of human control of systems and machines. It is this approach that we want to take into account here by appealing to the responsibility of humans for shaping the context of their lives.

Initiating the Paradigm Shift Now

It may be striking that we have given relatively little space to pointing out the negative and obstructive forces that effectively prevent a paradigm shift from happening. This can be justified by our conviction that paradigm shifts cannot be talked into people, nor can they be commanded. A paradigm shift comes about, when circumstances and the right people come together at the right time, when forces join forces to create something new.[44] We must learn to understand that these are processes that intervene deeply in the human being and finally mean profound changes for our cultures.

---

[44] In modern physics, a paradigm shift has been carried out in a period that began in the last decades of the 19th century, from Maxwell to Boltzmann and Mach, and which in the 20th century extended through the periods of Einstein, Bohr, Heisenberg to Pauli, and concluded with the formulation of modern quantum theory. This paradigm shift in physics was difficult to achieve and took time until it was finally accepted by all the people involved. Tobias Hürter has well traced this process of blurring in his book "The Age of Blurring (1895-1945)", from 2021.

In the social sphere, the 20th century was the most violent in human history[45]. The 21st century seems to be following this trend. The retarding and destructive forces have gained the upper hand in our societies and do not yet want to give way. Norbert Wiener had already warned against this in his socially critical work "The Human Use of Human Beings: Cybernetics and Society", in which he refers to the necessity of human control over systems and machines. Norbert Wiener says it clearly and unequivocally: people cannot avoid taking responsibility for their actions, and must always take responsibility for their future. It is this approach that we want to take into account here by appealing to the responsibility of us humans for shaping the context of our own lives and those of our fellow creatures. No excuse, no escape, we are all challenged here.

Even though we know that it is not always easy to initiate and carry out paradigm shifts, we must not back down from our responsibility. Paradigm shifts require a lot of courage and time to implement them, until

---

[45] The War of the World: History's Age of Hatred, from Niall Ferguson, 1st Edition, 2009, Penguin.

they are finally accepted by all the people concerned. We must learn to understand that these are mostly processes that intervene deeply in the human being and mean profound changes for our cultures.

In the 21st century, we should summon up the necessary courage a new and not let up in invoking the good forces and also showing ways, in which a quantum leap through a paradigm shift in geopolitics can lead to a world, where peaceful and sustainable progress are given priority for a qualitative improvement in the quality of life for people and their nations.

PART TWO - THE EMERGING NEW SYSTEM OF GLOBAL GOVERNANCE[46]

"The vast majority of humanity is of course its non-Western part, and the paradox is that we people of the West are people whose view of history often resembles that of the time before Vasco da Gama. Personally, I do not believe that this antediluvian, traditional conception of history of the West will last much longer. I have no doubt that a reorientation is imminent, and in our case it will, I think, be a reorientation in the literal sense of the word."

Unification of mankind and its world-political future
in: Outlook on the Future, anthology, 1968
Arnold Toynbee

---

[46] For a quick introduction to the topic, we recommend Helmut Willke's "Global Governance, 2006. Michael Zürn with "A Theory of Global Governance, Authority, Legitimacy, and Contestation", 2018.

Introduction

In this chapter of the book, we will show how the emerging new system of "global governance"[47] will change in the medium and long term due to China's economic rise and increasing political importance. There will be a paradigm shift in the functioning and interaction of the countries and nations of the earth. A new system of global governance is already emerging.

We are aware that this part of the book would deserve to be further expanded in scope and depth. We recommend that the work be undertaken in due course as part of a larger research program, perhaps led by the Berggruen Institute[48] as a neutral platform, in cooperation with universities from different

---

[47] We use the English term "Global Governance" throughout, which is also commonly used in the German-speaking world. In German, this would be called "global governance", or "rules-based global order beyond the nation state". The Berlin Social Science Center (WZB) offers a blog on this subject: https://www.wzb.eu/de/forschung/internationale-politik-und-recht/global-governance.

[48] https://berggruen.org/

countries and researchers from different cultural sectors.

Our outline will serve its purpose if it sufficiently demonstrates the need for a paradigm shift in the field of global governance. The essential trains of thought developed in this context are also intended to clearly show the contours of the current challenges. The contours that will appear in the course of our analytical description may also serve the purpose to provide a distinct orientation for future research.

It should have become clear by this point that we take a consistent reference to cybernetics in this book. As a consequence, we also intend to highlight the challenges we face, while at the same time providing useful guidance for the formulation of new rules according to which the coming system of global governance might function.

As a starting point and for the purpose of orientation, we would like to introduce this part of the book with <u>a working hypothesis,</u> pretending that *further global geopolitical development will not develop in a linear sequence*. If the system of global governance is to work and meet with the approval of the majority of the countries and nations involved, then the rules for its functioning must be changed. The hegemonic system of global governance that we have witnessed for more than a century, with the principle of armed conflict as the main political tool, will no longer be able to function. *The main reasons for this are of cultural origin.*

In my ideas and line of thinking, I have partially been inspired by the discussion of imperialism that has been going on in Germany for decades, initiated by the publications of Hannah Arendt.[49] A number of other important sources were also consulted.[50]

---

[49] Recommend reading: Hannah Arendt: The Origins of Imperialism in: The Hidden Tradition. Eight Essays, 1976. Further recommended reading: "The Origins of Totalitarianism". Furthermore "The Human Condition".

[50] On the Political Relevance of Historical Theories. The Imperialism Discussion in the Shadow of the Cold War, Federal Agency for Civic Education, Issue ApuZ 20/1972, Author: Timothy W. Mason.

Recommended reading: The Age of Imperialism (in Oldenbourg, Grundriss der Geschichte, Volume 15). 4th edition. Munich, 2000, by Gregor Schöllgen. (excellent, comprehensive and research-oriented

However, I derive the essential rationale for my hypothesis from my own long-term observations, studies and reflections on the subject.

The direct reason for the specific approach chosen within this essay on the topic of the paradigm shift in global governance was taken from the work of Stefan Schmalz[51], who repeatedly refers to the peculiarities of the "succession arrangement" within the previous capitalist order. The process of formation of the capitalist order, as it has been described by Fernand Braudel and approved by most scholars since then[52], took

---

overall presentation with 1223 literature references on various individual topics).

51 Schmalz, Stefan (2015): China's New Role in Global Capitalism. In: Prokla 40 (4):483-503.

Schmalz, Stefan/Ebenau, Mathias: Auf dem Sprung – Brasilien, Indien und China, 2011.

The Role of China in the Current Disputes about the Operational Mode of Globalization, in: Journal of International Relations, Vol. 25 (2018) Issue 2, pp. 144 – 163, Jenny Simon.

52 See h. Fernand Braudel Histoire et Sciences sociales : La longue durée, in : Annales, Année 1958, pp. 725-753.

place along a line of development with three striking steps: a) origin in Italy, during and as a result of the Renaissance; b) then rapid and globalizing further development led by several European states, until the formation of the dominant role of the British Empire in the 17th and 18th century; and finally c) after the end of the British Empire and the Victorian era in 1901, the takeover of the system and its principal results by the United States, with a following systematic consolidation and development of its political and economic mechanisms and with a continuous increase in dynamism up to the present time.

While these three major steps are considered essential, we could also name a multitude of intermediate stations and meanders in this history, which were often very important in

---

German: „Die lange Dauer". in: Schriften zur Geschichte, Bd. 1: Gesellschaft und Zeitstrukturen. 1992, pp. 49–87. Very important in our context is "The History of Civilization from the 15th to the 18th Century, 1982, Fernand Braudel. Original as "La dynamique du capitalisme. Paris, 1985. German as: The Dynamics of Capitalism. 2nd edition. 1991.

promoting this whole movement of capitalism over the past six centuries.

We would like to point out at this point a very important point that is characteristic of this movement and development of capitalism[53]: this kind of "capitalist civilization" was of European origin and driven by Europe.

With the re-entry of China as a player in world history[54] since the end of the 20th century, this situation has changed dramatically, especially since China's dynamic economic rise, which was initiated under the reign of Deng Xiaoping towards the end of the 20th century.

---

[53] We use the term "capitalism" here in a comprehensive sense that includes the different dimensions of social, political and economic action. So we are talking about a "global development process" of capitalism.

[54] There are now numerous studies and books on the topic of China's "new" entry into the active shaping of world history. We will only mention "The New Silk Roads, Present and Future of our World" by Peter Frankopan, 2018. This book also introduces the history of the Silk Roads, i.e. the period of development of trade relations and cultural exchange between Orient and Occident.

At this point, it might be useful to further clarify our initial working hypothesis putting it into the right global context: Since China belongs to a different cultural area[55] than the Western countries, the further development of global capitalism, and in particular of the new system of global governance, will not remain one-dimensionally European, and will thus not follow a linear path. There is a paradigm shift to occur.

We should also mention here that in recent decades, India has become an increasingly important player on the world political stage. India will certainly also have a say in the future structure and mechanisms of the system of global governance. But while India is still searching for its role in this global power game, China has already established itself as a major player.

---

[55] By using the word "culture", we do not want to limit the scope of related research to "cultural studies". Rather, we are concerned with opening up a field of scientific, historical research and philosophical reflection for research on the topic of global governance, which should encompass a wide range of relevant topics and areas.

Oswald Spengler predicted this necessary paradigm shift in his detailed introduction to his book "The Decline of the West"[56], where he elaborated on this issue in some detail. Spengler refers to other cultural areas that he does not assign to the Occident, i.e. to the West. This includes the Arab world, but also Russia and Latin America. We would also like to include Africa in this extension of the global scope, whose cultural power and importance are still not understood and whose potential impact on the shaping of future global systems is fundamentally underestimated.

In the further course of our analytical presentation, we will show, why the further geopolitical development will not be linear, and why the new system of global governance will follow new rules. We will also make it clear why the main reasons for this are of cultural origin.

---

[56] Spengler, Oswald; Der Untergang des Abendlandes, erster Band 1918, zweiter Band 1922. English: "The Decline of the West"

THE CULTURAL FOUNDATIONS OF CAPITALISM

In order to substantiate our hypothesis and to help it to be well understood, we must at least briefly include present the cultural background of global political and economic developments in our considerations. The background, on which this development of modern capitalism has taken place is on the one hand of a political and social nature, and on the other hand it arises to a decisive extent from scientific and technical development in Europe.[57]

There is an infinite number of studies and books on the social, economic and political prerequisites for the formation of the "modern world" and capitalism[58]. Most of them refer to a "secularization" as an essential event in the spiritual realm, i.e. an increasing awareness of the "absence of god"

---

[57] We refer here to "The Renaissance, the Reformation and the Rise of Nations", an audiobook in the series "The Great Courses" produced by "The Teaching Company", from 2005, by Andrew C. Fix.

[58] For an introduction to the topic, we recommend "The Renaissance, the Reformation and the Rise of Nations (1348 – 1715)", 2005, by Andrew C. Fix.

and of man's personal responsibility for the shaping of his living conditions. The German sociologist Max Weber has linked this to the "disenchantment of the world". On the more practical side, the development of the modern monetary system has been one of the most critical aspects of the naissance of modern capitalism, as the British historian Niall Ferguson, among others, has worked out clearly and in detail[59]. Let us tentatively call this aspect of the process the tendency toward the general "commercialization of the lifeworld". A third important prerequisite has been the increasing "juridification" of private and public life, which goes hand in hand with the development of the contractual system and the determination of the individual person as the bearer of rights and obligations.

However, beyond these various social aspects, the decisive foundations for the emerging form of capitalism in Europe during the Renaissance have been provided by scientific and technical development. Science and technology have challenged the

---

[59] By Niall Ferguson, The Ascent of Money, 2008. Of course, there are also numerous other good studies on this topic of the money economy.

European societies in an unprecedented way, and the answers to these challenges have led to completely new forms of human, anthropomorphic environments. Individuals and societies have taken up the challenges and have done their best to take advantage of the new opportunities and to adapt to the new requirements that have arisen again and again. The rapid progress of science and technology since the Renaissance and the subsequent Age of Enlightenment has led to a fundamental change in the worlds of life in all areas. This scientific and technological progress has developed faster and faster, with a conspicuous momentum of its own. Historically, this development of scientific and technological progress in Europe has been dynamized since the Middle Ages with the use of watermills and windmills, then continued after the Renaissance with the construction of mechanical looms and finally the development of the steam engine, then continued with the production and use of electrical energy in industrial production and for the construction of increasingly complex, later also self-controlling machines. In our days, these scientific and technological developments have led to the construction of automobiles, airplanes, nuclear power plants, satellites and spacecraft, and have finally conquered all areas of life with modern communication technology and social media. This development has now become global and seems to be inexorably following a forward-looking, very dynamic vector in today's world with the use of robotics and AI. This is only commonplace today, and no one will seriously want to deny the revolutionary significance of these science- and technology-driven developments for humanity.

We also agree that economic development has already made extensive use of this potential of modern science and technology and will continue to use it for its further development in the future. In view of current developments, this is also commonplace. The reason for this is the universality of scientific laws, what Buckminster Fuller calls "universal principles". At this point and as a reminder, we would like to briefly point out the universal principle of feedback, as it is understood in cybernetics, in its relevance for human-driven systems, i.e. societies. There, communication and observation are seen as the basic human competencies and system-theoretical functions that are used in the control of machines as well as in the design of societies.[60] The dynamic interplay of these basic human competencies and system-theoretical functions is feeding the further dynamics of scientific and technological progress. The universal principles are responsible for the linearity and cumulative mode of this development.

It is at this point, that we come in with our approach of a non-linear development of some specific mechanisms of global capitalism. Cultures do not follow the universal principle of causality or the laws of thermodynamics in their development. Relations between states follow rules as we know them from game theory, i.e. of movements within a system of correlations and dynamic relationships. Such systems not only depend on physical power and energy

---

[60] In this regard, we recommend the article by Arthur Koestler "Beyond Atomism and Holism – The Concept of Holon", in Das Neue Menschenbild. Revolutionizing the Sciences of Man", 1970, ed. Arthur Koestler and J. R. Smythies.

but also very much on human "willpower,"[61], as we have learned already in the early days of the 20th century from scientific research on self-regulating systems. Global governance is therefore about open relationships and the interaction of actors with different ideas and interests. Causal laws cannot be applied here, or only to a very limited extent, in strategic models or simulations. Therefore, the new system of global governance will not evolve in line with a linear system driven by the accumulation of power, as is the case with energy in the field of science and technology. In this area of global governance, which is crucial for the geopolitical organization on our planet Earth, a paradigm shift will have to take place through the development and application of new, commonly shared rules.[62]

---

[61] In the writings of Alwin Mittasch, former research director of BASF, Germany, we find enlightening reflections on the relationship between "Katalytische Kraft, Lebenskraft, Willenskraft" (our translation: *Catalytic energy, life energy, willpower*), p. 285 ff., Von der Chemie zur Philosophie, 1948. (our translation: *From Chemistry to Philosophie*).

[62] We agree with authors such as Helmut Willke, Global Governance, 2006, that this transformation of the system of global governance has to do with the emergence of a "knowledge society". In our

The hierarchies will concern the set of rules organizing the new system of global governance. This is what we learn from cybernetics and our knowledge of self-regulating systems. One-sided dominance built on political, financial and economic power cannot hold anymore.

The new system of global governance will emerge not in a linear sequence from the previous, European-dominated pattern, nor will it follow the European model in the sense of a causal relationship. Other factors from other cultures will come into play, so that this new system of global governance will eventually take on a new structure and form, regulated by a new set of rules agreed upon by the participating actors in this system.

At this point, one could add in a striking way that Protestant capitalism and Confucian-influenced capitalism get along relatively well and perhaps even seem to complement each other quite well, as far as we limit ourselves to

---

understanding, however, "knowledge" will not become an "instance" that could replace "law" as the authority in the decisions on how to function.

observing economic, productive and scientific-technical developments.

But things will be different with the system of global governance, i.e. the regulation of mechanisms, institutions and organizations of international cooperation. For the successful and peaceful cooperation of countries and nations within the "*global society*", new rules will have to be found and put into effect in order to enable a prosperous coexistence of people on our planet in the long term.

The maximization of economic utility as a principle of liberal capitalism, with its emphasis on individualism and the formation of hierarchical systems and structures, which in turn obey the principles of dominance and domination, will not remain valid in their current form in the field of global governance. The European model of global governance, which is based on power and money as the decisive instances, as well as on the all-pervasive rule of *the winner takes it all*, will be supplemented by other forms in the relatively near future, and will probably be replaced by a completely new concept of global governance in the distant future. This is how our understanding of the upcoming paradigm shift concerning global governance can be summarized at this point.

An important role in these considerations is played by the "succession arrangement", i.e. the "handover" of the previous form of capitalism, i.e. the domination through power and money, to the respective succeeding nation. This "handover" has so far followed a linear pattern as long as it has taken place within the European and Western worlds. In this linear handover to the continuation of the capitalist system on a new "higher" level, progress within Europe and later also in the USA was brought about by the addition of new and innovative elements and components. As long as this "handover" is carried out within the same cultural area, in which largely identical rules apply, progress could take place along a direct and comprehensible line, i.e. linearly.

To put it simply, these succession arrangements among European powers have taken the following steps leading to higher stages of capitalist efficiency: starting with the commercial capitalism of Venice and the capital formation through robbery, theft and extraction of gold and silver from South America by Spain and Portugal, the Netherlands has added a sophisticated monetary and an innovative financial system as driving forces. England has reshaped this system through the "indirect rule", i.e. a civilized form of colonialism (as opposed to mainly brute Spanish-Portuguese approach) and added Manchester capitalism on the production side, i.e. the value-adding processing of raw materials, often with the extensive use and brutal exploitation of human productive power. The British financial system represented essentially a continuation and improvement of the Dutch central and banking system. When the British system, which in the meantime had become a general European colonialism, collapsed because of the "imperialism of others", especially Germany, the USA took over the essential elements of the British system and supplemented them with Ford capitalism (consumptive production and "prosperity for all") and the forced further expansion through military dominance.

This linear sequence of capitalist development is largely unbroken, as long as it concerns only a certain cultural area, both in the area of social organization and in the development of science and technology. The effects of this cumulative development can be seen by the still existing domination of Anglo-American financial conglomerates.

China initially had no choice, but to fit into this linear development scheme with the aim of its economic development. Thus, within the scope of its own possibilities, the development of socialist "Shenzhen capitalism" was[63] initiated in order to open up new perspectives for the country. We all would agree that this initiative has been very successful overall. For the time to come, capitalist development in China can be expected to follow the European, linear-cumulative model in the field of economic development, because it is building on the potential of scientific and technological progress.

---

[63] "Shenzhen – Future Made in China: Between Creativity and Control", 2021, Frank Sieren. Or "Future? China!: How the new superpower is changing our lives, our politics, our economy", 2020, Frank Sieren, Josef Vossenkuhl, et al.

However, we encounter a different situation, when it comes to the regulation of social coexistence, or the regulation of interstate relations, i.e. international relations. If we enter a new cultural sphere to regulate international relations, then the linearity of development applies only to economic development and trade. This linearity of development no longer applies to the area of social development and to the system of global governance. Science and technology follow universal laws. Cultures, however, differ in the rules according to which they shape the coexistence of their members.

Transforming the System of Global Governance

According to our understanding, the economic development of capitalism will therefore follow the previous pattern for the time being.[64]

The situation is different, however, with global governance, which, according to previous understanding, is about the "struggle for power and money".[65]

As we mentioned in the first part of the book, dominance in capitalism, let's call it economic power, was explicitly tied to political and hegemonic power after the First World War, at the latest. This was already the case at the time of the British Empire, with its dominance over the seas and maritime trade, but after

---

[64] Refer to Immanuel Wallerstein, "The Capitalist World Economy, 1979. In "The Rise and Future Decline of the Capitalist World System, zur Grundlegung vergleichender Analyse. In: Senghaas Dieter (ed.): Kapitalistische Weltökonomie. Controversies about their origin and their development dynamics, 1979 and 1982.

[65] Money as financial strength, as potential to finance development.

1919, the USA made it a fundamental principle of its foreign policy. Since then, trade and international economic policy as well as security policy have always been closely interwoven.

It is also interesting to observe how a kind of "interregnum" occurred again and again. This is also pointed out by Stefan Schmalz in his work mentioned in the introduction. The subsequent stages in capitalist development were also characterized by learning processes and important adjustments. There was no existing blueprint that could have been followed exactly. When the USA adopted the Monroe Doctrine at the beginning of the 19th century, it did not yet know that 150 years later it would need the Bretton Woods system to secure and expand its global rule.

We want to clarify our reflections and give our considerations more emphasis, making a few comments on the "innovative pressures" that will arise in the current and intensifying transformation of the system of global governance. For this purpose, we want to make an insertion here that refers to research and considerations coming from historical science, but which also come from studies and sources on the "Particularity of Chinese Science" and "Scientific Universalism".[66]

There is already a comprehensive academic discussion on this topic of the transformation of the system of global governance[67], which we will not further discuss here. In our context, we would like to briefly refer to two important pioneers and original historians from Europe to make clear on what basis our considerations have grown.

To this end, we would first like to point out the connection between transformation and history. We have to realize that when we look at social transformations, we are moving in the "historical space of time". Therefore, we consider it indispensable to make a few comments clarifying our understanding of

---

[66] We refer here to the diverse and profound work of Joseph Needham in these areas. Under his direction, the Needham Research Institute has published a book series, "Science and Civilisation in China," on the history of science and technology in China since 1954.

[67] On this:
https://de.wikipedia.org/wiki/Global_Governance.
Then also in the German-speaking area:
https://www.wzb.eu/de/forschung/internationale-politik-und-recht/global-governance.

"time", at least to some extent, in order to arrive at a more comprehensive understanding of the ongoing transformation to the new system of global governance.

In this regard, we can glean Reinhart Koselleck many good and useful thoughts on the concept of time and "historical time".[68] In Christopher Clarke we see intelligent and further explanations of Koselleck's considerations, e.g. in his book "Time and Power".[69] From both scholars and authors, we can glean important thoughts on the concept of "time" in a historical context. In their studies and books, they demonstrate the importance of the different perceptions of the "historical space of time", i.e. historical time and space as the terrain for (geo-) political development, for the conception of political constitutions, the control of decision-making processes in countries and nations and the shaping of international relations. Their highly instructive considerations are mainly

---

[68] S. h. "Past Future. Zur Semantik geschichtlicher Zeiten", 1989, Reinhard Koselleck. "On the Semantics of Historical Times".

[69] "Of Time and Power", 2918, Christopher Clarke.

reflecting historical processes and events in the German and European area.[70]

However, for our concerns, we still have to supplement the considerations of these scientists and authors by lifting their fundamentally trend-setting understanding out of the European context. For in the future, Europe and its intellectual world will no longer be the exclusive global benchmark and the pattern, according to which the nations on our earth will shape their mechanisms and rules of coexistence. Oswald Spengler already points to this[71], when he warns of the "Ptolemaic system of history", in which "the high cultures make their rounds" around the "Western European", as "the supposed center of all world events". Even before the First World War, he foresaw that following the "Copernican discovery in the field of history... a system takes its place, in

---

[70] For France, the historian March Bloch has traced the historical birth of France in the space known as the hexagon with its social and economic structures in his masterpiece "The Feudal Society", new edition 2019, French original from 1939.

[71] In chapter 6 of the introduction to "The Decline of the West", original 1918, the quoted edition of 1922.

which antiquity and the West, along with India, Babylon, China, Egypt, and Arab culture, which as individual worlds weigh just as heavily in the overall picture of history,... do not occupy a privileged position in any way".

To supplement our argumentation, we would like to take up a very brief idea from organizational theory to insert a few additional useful reflections. in line with the general system approach in organizational development[72], the concept of culture has been common for a long time and different models are discussed in order to understand the meaning of "culture" in organizations[73]. There is general agreement that "core values" and "beliefs" determine how the world is seen

---

[72] Donella H. Meadows writes in her classical book "Thinking in Systems": A system is a set of things — people, cells, molecules, or whatever — interconnected in such a way that they produce their own pattern of behavior over time.

[73] For an introduction, we suggest reading "Understanding Organizational Culture: A Systems Theory Perspective", 2023, by Markus Perry. A more comprehensive understanding can be gained in: Kreitner, R. & Kinicki, A.; Organizational behavior, 2004, New York: McGraw-Hill.

and how life in it is considered best and most meaningful. In German, this is often referred to as "Weltanschauung", i.e. the particular way in which things, people and the world are seen in the context. These "basic values" and "beliefs" can be shaped very differently depending on the culture. Such a culturally shaped form of organization is often referred to as a paradigm, i.e. as a special social form with certain values and rules that have arisen historically. There is also agreement that these forms of organization must adapt to constantly changing circumstances and pressures from the environment, but also caused by the behavior of the internal actors of the system, in order to survive. So there are always changes, without which no system can survive. This is a well-known principle from cybernetics and general systems theory.[74]

---

[74] In an essay by Niall Ferguson, which was published in the NZZ on 31.12.2021 under the title "A nation is not an individual, and an individual is not a nation", he dispels in a convincing way one of the oldest ideas in Western political thought, which assumes an analogy between the individual human being and the political body of society. In the same sense, we reject the analogy between scientific and technological progress and social development.

In the current situation, the system of global governance is particularly exposed to such innovative pressure to adapt. The constantly blazing and flaring up of wars and conflicts contradict the principles of economic efficiency, for the majority of countries and nations on earth. Only a few countries are the winners and are drawing profits of wars and conflicts. On the other side, most of the countries and their peoples are paying a high price. Unipolar and hegemonic strategies cannot be justified from the perspective of a global world and the claim to peaceful settlement of the coexistence of nations. At the same time, such strategies are counterproductive in the sense of a sensible approach to the environment on earth, which is not divisible and will remain the basis of life on our planet.

It can further be learned from organizational theory, which has been shaped by systems theory, that a paradigm shift will occur, when an existential threat to an organization occurs, i.e. when the system is fundamentally endangered. In our understanding, such a threat to "Spaceship Earth", a term coined by

Buckminster Fuller, can[75] no longer be denied. Humanity is therefore faced with the challenge of developing a new paradigm, a new form and new rules for the system of global governance. In the sense of cybernetics, it can be assumed that neither the necessary processes can be fully planned, nor that the results will be predictable. This is a typical case of an "open system" as described and elaborated in detail by Karl Popper in the years after the Second World War[76]. Hence, such a step requires commitment for the future of humanity and life on earth.

---

[75] "Operating Manual for Spaceship Earth", 1969, by Buckminster Fuller. "Instruction manual for the spaceship Earth", German translation.
[76] "The Open Society and its Enemies", 1945. German edition in 2 volumes, "Die offene Gesellschaft und ihre Feinde", 1957 and 1958, by Karl Popper.

THE FUTURE SYSTEM OF GLOBAL GOVERNANCE: THE CULTURAL BACKGROUND

Our task here is not to discuss theories of global governance, i.e. to present possible models. However, we would like to point out here that all the discussions that are being held on this topic in the Western scientific field are fundamentally short-sighted, if they do not take into account and include the knowledge and lessons to be learned from the living traditions of other cultures.

We understand that knowledge and its availability will be hugely important in these discussions about determining a future system of global governance. But we do not assume that the current logic of power dominating global political governance will eventually be replaced by a logic of knowledge[77]. Both, power as well as knowledge, are not following logic. At the same time, there will probably not be a global legislature, functioning as a central legislative

[77] We refer here to "Global Governance", 2006, by Helmut Willke, who discusses the potential of knowledge for the system of global governance.

authority, that will prescribe that all people obey and function according to the same law[78]. There will probably be collectively binding rules, perhaps rules of conduct or principles, but no collectively binding law.[79] As we all know, the law has to be interpreted and does not function automatically. Hence, culture will again come into play to interpret laws in their specific context. We assume that at the level of global governance, everything will be decided according to the rules of discourse, i.e. rules that control communication and decision-making processes. At the national level, the legislature may continue to determine policy, but at the global level, different rules will have to apply. Nor will international organizations be able to take on executive functions. The international community will

---

[78] Even with a new assessment of "law" as a means of controlling action, we should recognize that the coming changes will pose a major challenge for the West.

[79] Stephen R. Covey presented such a principle-driven behavioral model in his bestseller "The 7 Ways to Effectiveness", original from 1990, German 1996. There he also speaks of the need to initiate a paradigm shift in thinking and acting.

be able to delegate mandates for the implementation of decisions to international organizations. However, they will not be given permanent executive functions. The experience of the WHO, IMF and World Bank has shown that international organizations are inclined to lead a life of their own due to pressure or incentives from their "hierarchical masters", from private and public "pay masters", or from big business and lobby associations. This means that international organizations will always tend to escape the control of the system of global governance. It is mainly for this reason that no executive functions should be delegated to them.

It will not be enough to expand the resources of the politics of power and power-based decisions beyond money to include the resource of knowledge. Values are culture based and can therefore not be used for politically successful control through the system of global governance in the context of world society and knowledge society. Obviously, subsidiarity and the authority for decision-making at the local and regional level will be required features. Ironically, this has been part of the political approach of the

EU under Jacques Delors. However, it did not fit into the expectations for "efficient leadership" of the US-hegemon and was only applied, as long as it did not contradict U.S. interests. The limitations of current proposals for the coming system of global governance lie in the fact that the Western social sciences and humanities are currently still under the influence of orthodox methodological and conceptual individualism, i.e. one decides for the others. They cannot imagine, or do not want to accept, that global networks and culturally differentiated conditions require new rules to govern them. Only under this premise will the new system of global governance be able to bring to a bearing the effectiveness of collective intelligence according to integrity and generalized patterns of human communication, as known from cybernetics.

The challenge of creating a new system of global governance is already well understood in China. There is now a broad, open and lively discussion about this, but it is largely conducted by the Chinese and in China. The Berggruen Institute promotes this discussion in China by funding an open scientific platform. In Germany, Richard Wilhelm commented on this Chinese challenge very early on[80]. British historians, such as Arnold J. Toynbee in his "Study of History", have also taken into consideration other cultures, but mostly with limited access to scientific literature from China. In the current Chinese discussion, Zhao Tingyang stands out with his presentation of "Tianxia"[81] as a potential model of future global governance .

From our perspective, the decisive contribution from Western science comes from Joseph Needham. In his writings and books on "Scientific Universalism" already mentioned, he has published an essay entitled "Time and Eastern Man". Needham

---

[80] e.g. in his little booklet "Wisdom of the East", from 1951.

[81] German edition "Everything under One Sky: Past and Future of the World Order,", 2019, Zhao Tingyang. ZHAO first tried to explain the concept of Tianxia in more detail in a monograph in 2005. In this book, there is a detailed bibliography on the subject. In January 2016, a new version of his Tianxia theory was published (Tianxia de dangdaixing: Shijie zhixu de shijian yu xiangxiang 天下的当代性:世界秩序的实践与想象, Zhongxin chubanshe).

writes: "I believe that I can show that the 'man of the West' did not have a monopoly on the sense of linear, continuous time, and that the idea of the 'timeless Orient' is nonsense[82]. In this essay on the "Concept of Time in the Orient", Joseph Needham has presented a comprehensive overview based on a detailed study of the relevant sources. It is not our intention to reproduce this presentation in detail here. The essence of his statements, however, seems to us important and essential for the argumentation we put forward here.

It does indeed seem to be the case that Chinese thought and culture, which has been shaped in China for 3000 years, is strongly fed by a source of synthetic[83] perception and

---

[82] Quoted from "Scientific Universalism", 1979, Joseph Needham, from the chapter "The Concept of Time in the Orient", pp. 176-250.

[83] An introductory discussion on understanding synthetic thinking vs. of analytical thinking can be found in the book on legal theory by Prof. Mahlmann, University of Zurich, which clearly presents "Basic Philosophical Teachings". https://www.rwi.uzh.ch/elt-lst-mahlmann/rechtstheorie/kant/de/html/unit_u2.html.

A basic presentation of the questions on analytical and synthetic thinking can be found in "Grundlagen der

understanding of things and processes. Opposites are not a problem in principle, but are seen as a challenge to find what they have in common, or even to see how such opposites can coexist in a complementary way and perhaps even complement each other fruitfully.

In this way, Needham shows that China asks us to take a differentiated view of the concept of "time", in which not all processes are linear. In the aforementioned essay on the "Concept of Time in the Orient", Needham addresses the question that is crucial for our concerns in a special chapter on "Time and History in China and the West". In the synopsis of Needham's studies on the "concept of time in the Orient", we learn that three dimensions of time can be distinguished in China, each of which was applied to specific areas:

- In the field of natural sciences, in China, as in the West, the "linear view of time" applies;

Systems Theorie", 1989, by Heinz Neubauer. Further information on this topic: https://de.wikipedia.org/wiki/Systemtheorie.

- In the area of society and state, a time is essentially oriented towards the social traditional rites. Marcel Granet[84] calls this the "liturgical" time. We would prefer to call this understanding of societal and social time "publicly organized time," or in a more modern and holistic wording the "time of rites, rhythms, and rituals";

- A third concept of time is "cyclical time", which results from the observation of nature and the understanding of the processes and the evolution of events in nature and in the cosmos.

It is not really difficult to understand, when looking at these three different concepts of time, that there is a big difference between the Chinese and the Western cultural sphere in the understanding of the passage of time in the social sphere.

---

[84] Marcel Granet, "The Chinese Civilization. Volume 2: Chinese Thought. Content, Form, Character", 2019. First published in German in 1985. Original: "La pensée chinoise", Paris, 1938.

In the West, the concept or understanding of linear time is applied in a rather one-sided and generalized way, not only to the natural sciences, but also to the understanding of the organization of societies and economic life[85]. Even regarding cosmic evolution, Western scientists will raise the question, when it started and how it will end. A cyclical approach to time seems not part of the Western scientific mind set. In the West, societies are always expected to focus on progress. The aim is to achieve results that are as quantifiable as possible.

Obviously, our politicians and leading elites did not yet learn the lessons of modern physics and natural science. If they had done this, they could have learned quite some time ago, that in catalytic processes there is often

---

[85] On April 11, 2022, the Mises Institute published an article by Eduard Braun entitled "Pseudoliberal State Interventions and Neoclassicism. Thoughts on Homo Oeconomicus and the True Value of Things". There he shows how an "unrealistic image of man" must lead to irrational assumptions about human behavior.

From this alone, i.e. from a new assessment of "law" as a control of action, we should recognize that the coming changes will pose a great challenge for the West.

no experimentally defined beginning and no end. In quantum theory, we have to do with events, about which no data can be found and for which it can only be measured the situation before and the situation after a specific event, such as a quantum leap. The absolute requirement for quantifiable results is a concept that not be applied to social processes, such as decision-making in a global environment, as we have already been able to impressively demonstrate in the earlier chapters of our book. The concept of "happiness" as enshrined in the American Constitution has degenerated into a capitalist concept that is all about material progress. General well-being must be quantifiable under American capitalism[86], and is measured by GDP. Prosperity, well-being and quality of life are only to be regarded as secondary, if at all. Therefore, it can also be understood that

---

[86] Goethe put the following words into the mouth of Mephistopheles in his Faust II: Mephistopheles (at the court of the emperor): "By this I recognize the learned gentleman! What you don't feel is miles away from you; What you do not grasp, you lack completely; What you do not reckon you believe is not true; What you do not weigh has no weight for you; What you do not coin, that, you think, does not count."

the issue of "environment" and concern for it plays only a secondary role in American politics, behind utility and profit, which are the primary driving forces for human action in the sense of their capitalist doctrine.

We do not want to conclude these remarks without briefly referring to the example of India. The Berggruen Institute has been promoting research and studies on the topic of governance in India and China for decades. In an important and trend-setting publication, classical Chinese and Indian political philosophy and theories of the state are compared in their practice and implementation.[87] This anthology also presents models of political organization from the Indian cultural sector that are very different from those, we in the West consider to be the "right" or the "best". In this book, the limits of the current political thinking based on the model of "Eurocentric

---

[87] Bridging two Worlds, Comparing Classical Political Thought and Statecraft in India and China. The book was published in 2003 by the University of California Press in the "Great Transformations" series. Edited by Daniel A: bell, Amitav Acharya, Rajeev Bhargava, Yan Xuetong.

International Relations" are criticized explicitly and in a well substantiated manner.

With these indications, our preliminary anticipation of the need for new mechanisms and rules for the system of global governance becomes quite concrete. From now on, it will be important to intensify practice-oriented research according to known system-theoretical-cybernetic methods with the interest to open up new perspectives and viable paths to create innovative mechanisms and new rules providing orientation for the design of the coming system of global governance.

In this respect, the suppression of this topic and the inability to take up the related challenges constructively and creatively is quite remarkable, especially in continental Europe. Jürgen Osterhammel, who is considered an important German historian on the topic of globalization and the "Far East", concluded his reflections and remarks in an article in the FAZ in 2022 with the title "All under one sky" by stating that there is not much to gain from this Tianxia system. Because in the end, Osterhammel writes, hierarchical decision-making power is necessary. According to him, without a "boss", no system can function. This shows the helplessness, at least of German historians, but unfortunately also of German scientists in general and of the general public in Europe, which remains trapped in their usual one-sided European thought patterns.

It is therefore not surprising that the document published by the State Council of the Republic of China in September 2023, entitled "The Global Community of a Shared Future: China's Proposals and Actions", has practically been ignored. This document explicitly points out that the Chinese government sees *humanity at a crossroad*, i.e. the world at a *tipping point*. With an explicit reference to their deep roots *in history and cultural traditions*, the Chinese then dare to put forward a proposal for future paths, i.e. *a Blueprint for the Future* for discussion, in order to even consider the *Direction and Path*, which they think humanity should take. In conclusion, they also take the liberty of pointing out China's actions so far and their contribution to the formation of a "Global Community of a Shared Future". To us, this sounds like an invitation and an offer for open discourse about the future design of the common path for humanity. Unfortunately, such offers are not being taken advantage of in the newly proclaimed Euro-American age of ideologies, confrontations and wars. Geopolitical hegemonic striving cannot be justified in such open discourses. So, Europe and America prefer to stay away from the talks on these global platforms and keep quiet about them. Contributions are left to scientists, without concern for public life and without remarkable impact on the ongoing transformation of our societies.

Perspectives for the Coming System of Global Governance

It seems helpful and useful to us, if we at least briefly address some additional considerations and studies on the role of knowledge as a decisive factor for the future system of global governance. We take as a reference point for our brief analysis the short but clever book on Global Governance by Helmut Willke. In this book he asks, among other questions, whether the future global governance system will follow the pattern of a knowledge based system and how the impact of knowledge on the emerging global governance system could be appreciated. In examining the reflections made by Willke, we also want to shed light on the challenges for the coming system of global governance from the perspective of systems theory.

We can agree with Willke[88] when he says, that "Modern organizations and societies are in transition to knowledge-based systems. In addition to the traditional infrastructures of power and money, knowledge is becoming

---

[88] Willke, 2006, p. 142 ff.

increasingly important as a condition of operation and as a necessary control resource". We also think it is extremely clever, when he suspects that the "collective effect of knowledge... is transformed in the direction of control, i.e. in the direction of a targeted change of natural courses in the direction of projected purposes and improbable lines of development". The word "natural" does not seem to be the appropriate notion here, because the processes he refers to are organizational processes of societies, so they are not "natural", but man-made.[89] This is an important distinction to be made. Taking up our earlier reference to the work of Alwin Mittasch, we should call these societal processes initiated by catalytic willpower, not by chemical energy. These processes may even be strategically oriented, i.e. they imply decisions on goals and planned "lines of development". In any case, in reality, these processes will usually encounter two problems or meet constraints during their realization. On the one hand, it is not always

---

[89] For this distinction between "natural" and "man-made", he could have referred to Giambattista Vico and his "Nova scientia" from 1725.

the case that such societal processes will lead directly to the desired goal. Experience shows that this will often be the case in dynamic processes within societies, which we consider to be open systems in the sense of Karl Popper.[90]

The more important problem that such social processes faces, however, is often that they give themselves wrong rules, or are based on false assumptions and preconditions. This is particularly the case, when persons or nations with different cultures enter into debates about social or political processes. In such culture biased debates the actors refer to distinct value systems, which in most cases are not reflected and duly taken into consideration. This then means that the desired goals could not be achieved at all with the processes as they were systemically designed, because the differing underlying assumptions are not taken into account.

---

[90] The book "Closed Systems and Open Minds. The Limits of Naivety in Social Anthropology", 2017, by Max Gluckman, opens a highly interesting debate related to this topic from the perspective of "culture". Hence, it strongly supports our approach to the new system of Global Governance.

Knowledge alone does not help here, but it is about the application of knowledge through sensible rules for the design of culture sensitive processes.

At a higher level, the additional challenge arises, when it comes to translating the results of the processes into responsible actions that are guided by such culture biased principles and values. "Objective" knowledge does not exist *a priori*, but has to be based on joint decisions as the outcome of discursive processes. Hence, "objective" knowledge is what is to be considered as such and is guiding decisions taken with the intention to serve specific purposes. Knowledge on the design of social processes is practice-oriented. The rules for controlling these human-led processes must be found in open, domination-free communication[91]. The shaping of such relationships can only be meaningfully realized in free exchange and open discourse. Domination-free communication not only prohibits the use of violence to achieve goals, but also requires

---

[91] The basic concept for this was presented by Jürgen Habermas in 1981 in his book on the "Theory of Communicative Action".

the dismantling of hierarchical structures and power imbalances in communication and interpersonal relationships. Objective truth and knowledge, which are supposed to guide action, arise through agreement, not through the dictates of individuals or specific and "mighty" state actors.

We can agree with Willke, when he pretends that there is no "world society" yet. For us, however, this does not mean that we can also do without control or self-regulation in international relations. The nation states have given themselves different forms of organization, be it the familiar forms of "democracies" we are familiar with in the West, or other organizational structures such as the socialist state system, like that of China. The nation states, with their respective political systems, laws and programs, have instances, such as a legal system, as mechanisms for internal self-regulation at their disposal in order to establish a desired order based on the rule of law.

However, we are taking here the external perspective and our interest is in finding rules for managing relations between these nation states. This is the next important step for us to take in our analytical overview on the impact of knowledge on the emerging global governance system. The challenges inherent to open, self-regulating systems are coming to the fore, if we take the debate to this higher aggregate and more complex level, where consensus cannot be reached through coercion managed by a legal system. The global governance system is composed of a relatively high number of individual and interdependent state actors. For such a system a contingency approach is required recognizing that there is no universal management approach and the optimal approach depends on situational factors and a number of important constituent factors, such as culture, technology, demography, economy, government and geography. The challenge we are facing is to apply our knowledge about systems theory, as it is known by the natural sciences, to the organization of human action functioning as a cooperative system.

The sciences of chemistry and biology have shown that there are rules that regulate self-organizing systems. Such rules will have to be identified and agreed upon jointly for the new global governance system. These will be the overarching rules regulating the new global governance system as a self-regulating system. However, below this general level, the contingency approach applies, which requires us to admit that there are no universal rules that would apply to mechanical decision-making. A dominant or hegemonic attitude and behavior will pretend to know such rules, i.e. the generalized drive for economic profits or social effectiveness. However, cultures are providing space for humans to live their lives according to rules they agree upon. Cultures have been created as self-regulating systems, accepting contingency as one of their basic rules.

We therefore have to accept that contingency, i.e. the principle of chance, is not the critical "enemy" of such global systems and orders. Contingency only becomes an enemy, when political systems aim for stability and rigidity and are resisting change and adaptations to new situations. Of course, this also applies to the global world order. As history has sufficiently shown, all known political systems are in constant process of development. These developments can always be considered "contingent", because the future challenges can never be foreseen. To put it simply: contingency, i.e. chance, can never be completely eliminated in all areas of human life, so even man-made social systems of order must always live with the principle of contingency. On the positive side, contingency is usually linked to people's creativity. It is then to be regarded as a positive property of the systems, because they can only be further developed on the basis of human creativity.

The greatest challenge for the governance of a future system of global governance thus seems to us to stem from the cultural diversity in our "global village" i.e. the countries, states and nations. This cultural diversity has become "virulent", i.e. meaningful, through globalization. Humanity can no longer avoid this diversity. Hegemony, i.e. rule by one power, and not even by two or three powers, is no longer possible today. The reversal of the balance of power is already well advanced and is inexorably taking its course. This is certainly to be seen as a step forward in the development of mankind.

The "disenchantment of the world" has not turned humans into robots. Likewise, globalization has not led to neo-colonization, as the power elites in the USA and Europe might have wished for in order to further assert their claim to power. The "disenchantment has "woken humanity up" and made us aware that we can create their social systems of order under our own sovereign responsibility. As general systems theory and self-regulating systems teach us, we humans should take our responsibility consciously. As Alwin Mittasch tells us, will power is the catalytic energy within human systems. Hence, the conscious use of will power will be the catalytic power leading to the creation of the new system of global governance.

However, it will not be a matter of creating a unity out of the multiplicity, as Thomas Hobbes intended for his Leviathan, i.e. a "singular" system that will obey only the rules of one single participant, or even only the rules of a privileged group. Order through unity seems to make sense as a working principle for the functioning of nation states. However, the coming system of global governance must come to a new, open order benefitting from the influx of creativity through cultural diversity and political heterogeneity.

It seems appropriate to us to address at least briefly the topic and meaning of "collective intelligence," as well as "systems of self-organization", as they are known from biology. These terms come up again and again in the context of discussions on global governance. We do consider such discussions as useful, but will have to put these issues in the context of our analysis.

We would like to point out here that we consider "collective intelligence", as well as biological systems of self-organization,[92] to be very important and assume that people can learn a lot from it for the design of their own organizational systems. This also applies to the system of global governance. However, this does not mean that "collective intelligence" or biological systems of self-

---

[92] Prigogine, for example, speaks of "order through fluctuation". A conversation with Ilya Prigogine, 1979. But also the sciences of chaos theory, presented in "The Discovery of Chaos", 1997, John Briggs and F. David Peat are part of it.

organization can take on the function of instances of human control for decision-making processes within the system of global governance. It is important to integrate collective intelligence and knowledge of biological self-organization into the design of the decision-making processes of the future system of global governance. Both can be seen as instruments of reflection and can then contribute to overcoming the limits of "objective" knowledge. We also believe that both the understanding of collective intelligence and the knowledge of biological processes of self-organization are important. They can make an important contribution to the constantly improved regulation of the future system of global governance and to an increased quality of decision-making processes. Willke rightly points out that "the core of intelligence is the ability to learn" and then concludes just as correctly that "organizational intelligence" consists of "organizations as organizations, as social systems, learning." We agree with these assumptions. They will also have to apply to the system of global governance.

From the point of view of systems theory, it is certainly right to demand that a highly complex future system of global governance has the ability to take into account the diverse demands of the individual participants, i.e. to deal with the requirements of systemic complexity and cultural diversity, as well as with situations of disorder and heterogeneity.

We also see one of the crucial requirements that a future system of global governance must meet in "that the system is able to vary the form of decision-making depending on the specificity of the decision-making situation, without the variations overriding the basic rules of decision-making". [93] So we agree with Willke on this, and point out that his formulation "special nature of decision-making forms" already refers to the principle of diversity. However, he fails to point out the cultural moment. Willke is a sociologist, not a social anthropologist, like Gregory Bateson. Therefore, he overlooks the factor of "social culture", which will be decisive for the diverse demands of the participants in global decision-making processes. A future system

---

[93] Willke, p. 131 ff

of global governance must, by principle, be open. It is this principal openness of the system that will enable it to take into account the respective cultural backgrounds of the actors and participants.

So we agree again with Willke that for the international context of a future system of global governance, it will be a matter of creating a dynamic order under conditions of pronounced cultural diversity and "under conditions of high contingency". This dynamic order must also be based on the autonomy of the individual participants, i.e. sovereignty in the case of nations, and presupposes the willingness of the participants to self-restraint, mutual respect and understanding, as well as the will to take responsibility for decisions taken at the global level.

We also agree with Willke, when he suspects that law will lose its role as an overarching architecture for control of the system within the context of a global governance system. He presumes that the architecture of the regulatory systems for a coming system of global governance will have to become "richer, more diverse and more atopic".[94] The systems of rules themselves will have to adapt to new forms of order, such as global governance, which, as a complex form of order, will encompass a great cultural and political diversity of different participants and actors.

We are aware that, in the context of our analysis, we have only briefly looked at a number of important issues. In order to better understand the interdependencies and relationships, and to deepen their analytical understanding, further interdisciplinary and intercultural research will be necessary so that the questions raised, and the hypotheses mentioned can be answered more precisely and comprehensively in detail.

Other important and interesting topics could very well complete our analytical overview on global governance. We are thinking, for example, of the role of Europe and the EU in a multilateral system of global governance.

---

[94] "Atopia", from 2001, is the title of one of Helmut Willke's books, in which he presents the "form of a society that radically dissolves its territorial boundaries".

This is certainly an exciting topic, on which extensive research has been conducted, and many reports have been produced, albeit mostly with a Eurocentric bias. Hence, it is a big topic and would deserve to be dealt with scientifically in its own right and with a more nuanced approach, including issues of culture at a global level.

Bibliography

Abelshauser, Werner; Wunder gibt es immer wieder: Mythos Wirtschaftswunder, in: Aus Politik und Zeitgeschichte, 68 (2018) 27, S. 4-10.

Ansprenger, Franz; Auflösung der Kolonialreiche, 1989.

Armstrong, Karen; The Great Transformation: The Axial Age, 2005. Deutsch: Achsenzeit der grossen Zivilisationen, 2006.

Attali, Jacques; Biographie: C'était François Mitterand, Paris, 2007.

Bateson, Gregory; Geist und Natur. Eine notwendige Einheit, 1987.

Bateson, Gregory; in Ökologie des Geistes, Teil VI, Krisen in der Ökologie des Geistes, von Versailles zur Kybernetik, Vorlesung von 1966.

Bateson, Gregory; Ökologie des Geistes, 1985; English edition: Steps to an Ecology of Mind, Collected Essays, 1972.

Bell, Daniel A, Amitav Acharya, Rajeev Bhargava, Yan Xuetong (eds.); Bridging two Worlds, Comparing Classical Political Thought and Statecraft in India and China, 2003. University of California Press, series: Great Transformations.

Benjamin, Craig G.; Foundations of Eastern Civilization,

Berger, Jens; Wer schützt die Welt vor den Finanzkonzernen?, Frankfurt, 2020.

Bernstein, Richard J.; Beyond objectivism and relativism: Science, Hermeneutics, and Praxis, University of Pennsylvania Press 1983.

Bittner, Wolfgang; Die Eroberung Europas durch die USA, 2015.

Blankart, Charles B.; Föderalismus in Deutschland und in Europa, 2007, erschienen in der Reihe „Neue Studien zur Politischen Ökonomie", Nomos Verlag.

Blankart, Charles B.; Öffentliche Finanzen in der Demokratie: Eine Einführung in die Finanzwissenschaft, Gebundene Ausgabe, 2017.

Bloch, Marc; Die Feudalgesellschaft, Neuausgabe 2019, Französisches Original von 1939.

Bono, Edward de; Lateral Thinking: a Textbook of Creativity, 1970.

Bono, Edward de; Laterales Denken : Ein Kursbuch zur Erschliessung ihrer Kreativitätsreserven, 1971.

Bördlein, Christoph; Einführung in die Verhaltensanalyse (English edition: Introduction to Behavioral Analysis), 2015.

Born, Max; Der Mensch und das Atom, in: Ausblick auf die Zukunft, 1968.

Bozo, Frederic; Deux stratégies pour l'Europe, Paris, 1996.

Bracher, Andreas; Europa im amerikanischen Weltsystem, Bruchstücke zu einer ungeschriebenen Geschichte des 20. Jahrhunderts, 2001.

Bracher, Andreas; Völkische Selbstbestimmung und Dreigliederung, in der Zeitschrift Perseus, der Europäer, Jg. 6 Nr. 8, Juni 2002.

Brandt, Willy; Frieden sichern und Mauern überwinden – Ost- und Deutschlandpolitik 1955–1989. https://www.willy-brandt-biografie.de/politik/ost-und-deutschlandpolitik/

Braudel, Fernand; Die lange Dauer. in: Schriften zur Geschichte, Bd. 1: Gesellschaft und Zeitstrukturen. 1992, S. 49–87. Ganz wichtig in unserem Zusammenhang ist „Die Geschichte der Zivilisation vom 15 bis zum 18 Jahrhundert, 1982.

Braudel, Fernand; Histoire et Sciences sociales : La longue durée, in : Annales, Année 1958, pp. 725-753.

Braudel, Fernand; L'Identité de la France, auf Deutsch herausgegeben als «Frankreich, Band 1: Raum und Geschichte / Band 2: Die Menschen und die Dinge / Band 3: die Dinge und die Menschen, 2009.

Braudel, Fernand; La dynamique du capitalisme. Paris, 1985. Deutsch als: Die Dynamik des Kapitalismus, 1991.

Braun, Eduard; Pseudoliberale Staatsinterventionen und die Neoklassik . Gedanken zum Homo Oeconomicus und zum wahren Wert der Dinge, Mises Institute, Mises Wire, 11. April 2022.

Bricker, Darrell and Ibbitson, John; Empty Planet: The Shock of Global Population Decline, 2019

Briggs, John und Peat, F. David; Die Entdeckung des Chaos, 1997; das Original ist 1989 unter dem Titel „Turbulent Mirror" in New York veröffentlicht worden.

Brzezinski, Zbigniew, The Grand Chessboard: American Primacy and its Geostrategic Imperatives, 1997.

Brzezinski, Zbigniew; Die einzige Weltmacht: Amerikas Strategie der Vorherrschaft, 1999.

Burkhard, Jakob; Kultur der Renaissance in Italien, Erstveröffentlichung 1860.

Butterwegge, Christoph; Die zerrissene Republik. Wirtschaftliche, soziale und politische Ungleichheit in Deutschland, 2019.

Campbell, Joseph; Thou art That. Transforming Religious Metaphor. The spiritual meaning of Biblical Stories, Miracles and Parables, 2002.

Campbell, Joseph; Understanding and Interpretation of Mythology. The Website of the Joseph Campbell Foundation: https://www.jcf.org/.

Fritjof; Tao der Physik, 1977.

Carstens, Peter; Deutsch-Französisches Projekt: Ein Kampfflugzeug für 100 Milliarden Euro, in der FAZ vom 21.01.2020.

Carter, Robert; Frank Lloyd Wright, A Biography, 2006.

Chomsky, Noam; Sprache und Geist, 1970. Darin der Anhang aus *New Left Review* (Nummer 57, September/Oktober 1969).

Chomsky, Noam; Rules and Representations. Behavioral and Brain Sciences, 1980. . Deutsch: Regeln und Repräsentationen, 1980

Chomsky, Noam; Gespräch mit C. J. Polychroniou zum Thema „Warum China, nicht Russland die US-dominierte Weltordnung bedroht", auf Deutsch am 09.07.2022 in Telepolis; Original in Trouthout.

Chomsky, Noam; in Asia-Pacific-Forum vom 31.12.2012, Revenge Of History: Chomsky on Japan, China, The United States, And The Threat of Conflict in Asia".

Clark, Christopher; Die Schlafwandler: Wie Europa in den Ersten Weltkrieg zog, 2013.

Clark, Christopher; Von Zeit und Macht, 2918.

Club of Rome, Grenzen des Wachstums, 1962.

Couvée, Leonard; Verslumung als Folge von Metropolisierung, 2016.

Covey, Stephen R.; Die 7 Wege zur Effektivität, Original von 1990, deutsch 1996.

Dagdelen, Sevim; Die NATO: Eine Abrechnung mit dem Wertebündnis, 2024.

Dangeleit, Elke; Deutschland finanziert Erdogans Umsiedelungspolitik in Nord- und Ostsyrien, Online Magazin Telepolis, vom 24. Januar 2020.

Davis, Irvine Mike; Planet der Slums, Department of History an der University of California, 2005; Planet der Slums ist 2019 auf Deutsch erschienen.

Denson, John V.; "A Century of War" wurde 1997 als Vortrag zum fünfzehnjährigen Jubiläum des Ludwig von Mises Institute gehalten und Mises.org veröffentlicht.

Desjardins, T. ; François Mitterand: un socialiste gaullien, Paris, 1978.

Diamond, Jared; Guns, Germs and Steel. The Fates of Human Societies, 1998.

Doering-Manteuffel, Anselm; Amerikanisierung und Westernisierung, Version: 2.0, in: Docupedia-Zeitgeschichte, 19.08.2019.

Dresdener gesammelte Kommentare zur Sicherheitspolitik – dgksp-diskussionspapiere – vom 14. April 2021.

Duerr, Hans-Peter; Der Mythos vom Zivilisationsprozeß, 2005.

Conze, Eckart; Hegemonie durch Integration: Die amerikanische Europapolitik und ihre Herausforderung durch de Gaulle, in: Institut für Zeitgeschichte, Vierteljahreshefte für Zeitgeschichte, Jahrgang 43 (1995), Heft 2.

Egli, Rene; Das Lola Prinzip, Die Vollkommenheit der Welt, 1994.

Ehrlich, Paul R.; The Population Bomb,
New York: Ballantine Books 1968; dt.
Übers.: Die Bevölkerungsbombe, 1971.

Eksteins, Modris; Rites of Spring: The Great
War and the Birth of the Modern Age, 1989.

Evans, Richard; The Pursuit of Power, Europe
1815-1914, 2016.

Ferguson, Niall; Colossus: The Rise and Fall of
the American Empire, 2004.

Ferguson, Niall; Eine Nation ist kein
Individuum, und ein Individuum ist keine
Nation, am 31.12.2021 in der NZZ.

Ferguson, Niall; Empire: How Britain Made
the Modern World, 2003.

Ferguson, Niall; The Ascent of Money: A
Financial History of the World, 2008.

Ferguson, Niall; The Cash Nexus. Money and
Power in the Modern World, 1700–2000,
2001.

Ferguson, Niall; The War of the World: History's Age of Hatred, 1st Edition, 2009.

Fix, Andrew C.; The Renaissance, the Reformation and the Rise of Nations", Audible Audiobook series: „The Great Courses" produced by „The Teaching Company", 2005.

Focus Magazin Nr. 8, 2009; "Alles schon gelaufen?", Wem gehört Deutschland?

Foreign Affairs, Volume 103 Number 3, No Substitute for Victory, 2024. https://www.foreignaffairs.com/united-states/no-substitute-victory-pottinger-gallagher

Fortes, Meyer; The Political Systems of the Tallensi of the Northern Territories of the Gold Coast, in African Political Systems, M. Fortes and E.E. Evans-Pritchard (eds.), First Edition 1940.

Frankopan, Peter; The Silk Roads, The New History of the World, 2015.

Freud, Sigmund; Vorlesungen zur Einführung in die Psychoanalyse, 1917.

Friedrich, Marc und Weik, Matthias ; Komplette, legale Enteignung per Gesetz, 2019.

Fröhlich, Stefan; Die transatlantischen Beziehungen, Deutschland, 2017.

Fuller, R. Buckminster; Critical Path, 1981;

Fuller, R. Buckminster; Ideas and Integrities, 1963.

Fuller, R. Buckminster; Nine Chains to the Moon", 1938.

Fuller, R. Buckminster; Operating Manual for Spaceship Erath, 1969; deutsche Ausgabe: Bedienungsanleitung für das Raumschiff Erde und andere Schriften", 2011.

Gluckman, Max; The Limits of Naivety in Social Anthropology", 2017.

Goethe, J. W.; Faust, Tragödie Erster und Zweiter Teil, 1986.

Granet, Marcel; Die chinesische Zivilisation. Band 2: Das chinesische Denken. Inhalt, Form, Charakter, Ersterscheinung deutsch 1985. Original: „La pensée chinoise", Paris 1938.

Greene, Robert; Die Gesetze der menschlichen Natur, 2019; das englische Original „The Laws of Human Nature, 2018.

Greene, Robert; Gesetze der Macht. engl. The Laws of Power, 1998.

Grenoble University, Ecole de Management (GEM) de Grenoble, Energie for Society, Université de Grenoble, Politiques énergétiques : comment éviter une dystopie européenne?, 2024.
Griffin, George Edward; The Creature from Jekyll Island, 1994.

Grün, Arno; Dem Leben entfremdet, 2019.

Guelzo, Allen C., et al.; The History of the United States, 2003, 2nd Edition, 2013.

Guilford, J. P.; The Structure of Intellect, in Psychological Bulletin, Volume 53 N° 4, July 1956.

Habermas, Jürgen; Theorie des kommunikativen Handelns, 1981.

Hahn, Robert; Herrschaft von Lissabon bis Wladiwostok", 06.07.2022.

Hayek Friedrich A. v.; Weltwirtschaftliches Archiv, 36. Bd., 1932.

Hayes, Sam W. and Morris, Christopher (eds.): Manifest Destiny and Empire: American Antebellum Expansionism, 1997. Heer, Burkhard; Umwelt, Bevölkerungsdruck und Wirtschaftswachstum in Entwicklungsländern, 2013.

Hegel G.W.F.; Tagebuch der Reise in die Berner Oberalpen, 1796. In: K. Rosenkranz, G.W.F. Hegels Leben [1844]. Darmstadt 1969: 470–89.

Heinsohn, Gunnar; Söhne und Weltmacht, 1. Auflage 2005.

Heisterkamp, Jens (Hg.); Die Jahrhundertillusion. Wilsons Selbstbestimmungsrecht der Völker, Sammelband, 2002.

Hellmann, Gunther; Zwischen Gestaltungsmacht und Hegemoniefalle: Zur neuesten Debatte über eine neue deutsche Außenpolitik, in der Reihe „Aus Politik und Zeitgeschichte, 11.07.2016.

Heylighen, Francis; , Accelerating Evolution, 2007, in Modelski, Tessaleno and Thompson, William (eds.), "Globalization as an Evolutionary Process: Modeling Global Change", Rethinking Globalizations, London 2007.

Hobsbawm, Eric; Zeitalter der Extreme, Weltgeschichte des 20. Jahrhunderts, 1995.

Horkheimer, Max und Adorno, Theodor W.; Dialektik der Aufklärung, 1944.

Horsman, Reginald; Race and Manifest Destiny: The Origins of American Racial Anglo-Saxonism, 1981.

Hülsmann, Jörg Guido; Abundance, Generosity, and the State: an Inquiry into Economic Principles, 2024.

Hummel, Diana; Der Bevölkerungsdiskurs: Demographisches Wissen und politische Macht, 2000.

Hungary Today, Online Magazin vom 24. Mai 2024.

Hürter, Thomas; Das Zeitalter der Unschärfe, 2021.

Jordan, Pascual; Wie sieht die Welt von morgen aus?, 1958.

Jung, C. G.; Biographie: Erinnerungen, Träume, Gedanken, 1962.

Jung, C. G.; Modern Men in Search of a Soul", auf Deutsch „Der moderne Mensch auf der Suche nach einer Seele", von 1933.

Keynes, John Maynard; Krieg und Frieden: Die wirtschaftlichen Folgen des Vertrags von Versailles, 1920.

Koestler, Arthur and Smythies, J. R. (eds);
Revolutionizing the Sciences of Man, 1968.

Koestler, Arthur; Jenseits von Atomismus und
Holismus – Der Begriff des Holons, in, "Das
Neue Menschenbild – Die Revolutionierung
der Wissenschaften vom Menschen", 1970,
Hrsg. Arthur Koestler und J. R. Smythies.

Kohlenberg, Kerstin und Schieritz, Mark; am
23. Oktober 2014, in DIE ZEIT Nr. 44/2014,
Die Superwaffe des Mr. Glaser, Sanktionen
gegen Russland und den Iran: Wie
amerikanische Finanzbeamte zu
Wirtschaftskriegern werden.

Konersmann, Ralf (Hrsg.); Kulturkritik:
Reflexionen in der veränderten Welt, Reclam
2001.

Konicz, Tomasz; Türkei: Merkels
zivilisatorischer Tabubruch, Online Magazin
Telepolis, vom 25. Januar 2020.

Koselleck, Reinhard; Vergangene Zukunft.
Zur Semantik geschichtlicher Zeiten, 1989.

Kreitner, R. & Kinicki, A; Organizational Behavior, 2004, New York: McGraw-Hill.

Krohne, Heinz W.; Psychologie der Angst, 2010.

Kuhn, Thomas S.; The Structure of Scientific Revolutions, 1962.

Lau, Jörg; "Regelbasierte Weltordnung. In 80 Phrasen um die Welt", 01. Juli 2020.

Lee, Kuam Yew; From Third World to First, 2016.

Lévi-Strauss, Claude; Das wilde Denken, 1976.

Li Xuanmin and Fan Anqi; Government of China „White paper", in Global Times China, 19. Januar 2023, https://www.globaltimes.cn//author/Reporter -Li-Xuanmin.html.

Lieven, Dominic (ed.); The Cambridge History of Russia, 2005.

Lohmann, Sascha; in SWP-Aktuell 2019/A 31, Mai 2019, Extraterritoriale US-Sanktionen.

Lorenz, Konrad und Wuketits, Franz (Hg.): Die Evolution des Denkens. Zwölf Beiträge, 1983.

Lorenz, Konrad; Das sogenannte Böse: Zur Naturgeschichte der Aggression, 1963.

Lovelock, James; Gaia. A New Look at Life on Earth, 1972.

Lukács, Georg; Die Zerstörung der Vernunft, 1955.

Mackinder, Halford; Artikel „The Geographical Pivot of History, 1904.

Mahlmann, Matthias; Philosophische Grundlehren, 7. Auflage, 2022. https://www.rwi.uzh.ch/elt-lst-mahlmann/rechtstheorie/kant/de/html/unit_u 2.html.

Marschall, Tim; The Future of Gegography, 2023.

Mausfeld, Rainer; Warum schweigen die Lämmer?, 2018.

Mayer, Thomas; Die Ordnung der Freiheit und ihre Feinde: Vom Aufstand der Verlassenen gegen die Herrschaft der Eliten, 2018.

Meadows, H. Donella; Thinking in Systems, 2008.

Mereschkowski, Dmitri; Leonardo da Vinci, 1951.

Merk, Frederick; Manifest Destiny and Mission in American History: A Reinterpretation, 1963.

Mises, Ludwig von; Human Action: A Treatise on Economics, 1949.

Mises, Ludwig von; Theorie des Geldes und der Umlaufmittel, 1912.

Mises, Ludwig von; Vom Wert der besseren Ideen, Vorlesungen, 1958.

Mittasch, Alwin; Von der Chemie zur Philosophie, 1948.

Mohr, Daniel; „Viele amerikanische Investoren, Der Dax ist fest in ausländischer Hand", FAZ vom 26.01.2017.

Morland, Paul; The Power of Demography to Understand Our World, 2019.

Mumford, Lewis; The Original American edition: The Transformation of Man, 1956.

Mumford, Lewis; Mythos der Maschine. Kultur, Technik und Macht, 1986.

Mumford, Lewis; Technics and Civilization, 1934.

Mumford, Lewis; The Condition of Man, 1944.

Mumford, Lewis; The Culture of Cities, 1938.

Mumford, Lewis; The Story of Utopias, 1922.

Needham, Joseph; Moulds of Understanding, 1976.

Needham, Joseph; Needham Research Institute, Science and Civilisation in China, since 1954.

Needham, Joseph; Wissenschaftlicher Universalismus, 1979, das Kapitel „Der Zeitbegriff im Orient", s. 176-250.

Neubauer, Heinz; Grundlagen der Systemtheorie, 1989.

Nietzsche, Friedrich; Genealogie der Moral, 1887.

Pany, Thomas; Syrien-Krise und EU: Katastrophale Armut und Auswanderung als letzter Ausweg, 22. Februar 2024.

Perry, Markus; Understanding Organizational Culture: A Systems Theory Perspective, 2023.

Pfluger, Walter; Ronga – Ein Beispiel politischer Komplementarität, 1987.

Popper, Karl; The Open Society and its Enemies, 1945. Deutsche Ausgabe in 2 Bänden, „Die offene Gesellschaft und ihre Feinde", 1957 und 1958.

Prigogine, Ilya; Order through Fluctuation.
Self-Organization and Social System, 1976.

Reid, Anna; Borderland, A Journey Through
the History of the Ukraine, 2015.

Reinhard, Wolfgang; Die Unterwerfung der
Welt: Globalgeschichte der europäischen
Expansion 1414 – 2015, 2017.

Richard, Wilhelm; Weisheit des Ostens, von
1951.

Riemann, Fritz; Basic Forms of Fear. A depth
psychological study, 1975.

Richter, Horst-Eberhard; Flüchten oder
Standhalten, 2012.

Richter, Horst-Eberhard; Moral in Zeiten der
Krise, Originalausgabe 2010.

Riegel, Tobias; Syrien – Die unendliche
(Lügen-)Geschichte", 20. Februar 2020.

Riemann, Fritz; Grundformen der Angst. Eine tiefenpsychologische Studie. 10. überarbeitete und erweiterte Auflage, 1975.

Risk Management Network, Neue Ära der Großmachtkonflikte – Erosionsprozesse der geopolitischen Welt, am 7. Oktober 2019. https://www.risknet.de/themen/risknews/ero sionsprozesse-der-geopolitischen-welt/.

Rübel, Gerhard; Grundlagen der monetären Aussenwirtschaft, 2009.

Rügemer, Werner; Die Kapitalisten des 21. Jahrhunderts. Allgemeinverständliche Notizen zum Aufstieg der neuen Finanzakteure, 2018.

Rügemer, Werner; USA im Niedergang? – Aber in der EU so mächtig wie noch nie, Artikel im Online Magazin „Nachdenkseiten" vom 23. April 2019.

Sachs, Jeffry; Agenda der US-Aussenpolitik", am 20. Dezember 2023, auf dem Online Magazin Telepolis: https://www.telepolis.de/features/Kriegsdeba kel-und-viel-Geld-Die-geheime-Agendahinter-der-gescheiterten-US-Aussenpolitik-9584068.html?seite=all.

Sachs, Jeffry;
https://www.jeffsachs.org/newspaper-articles/

Sakwa, Richard; Frontline Ukraine: Crisis in the Borderlands, 2022.

Sakwa, Richard; The Lost Peace: How the West Failed to prevent a Second Cold War, 2023.

Sakwa, Richard; Wir sind an der Beerdigung der alten Schule der Diplomatie, Interview vom 21. Mai 2024 in GlobalBridge.

Schmalz, Stefan und Ebenau, Mathias; Auf dem Sprung – Brasilien, Indien und China, 2011.

Schmalz, Stefan; Chinas neue Rolle im globalen Kapitalismus. in: Prokla 40 (4):483-503, 2015.

Schöllgen, Gregor; Das Zeitalter des Imperialismus (in Oldenbourg, Grundriss der Geschichte, Band 15), 2000.

Schuldt, Christian; Zeitalter der Krisen, Bundesverband „Energie, Wasser, Leben", 2021.

Sieren, Frank und Vossenkuhl, Josef, et al; "Zukunft? China! Wie die neue Supermacht unser Leben, unsere Politik, unsere Wirtschaft verändert", 2020.

Sieren, Frank; Shenzhen – Zukunft Made in China: Zwischen Kreativität und Kontrolle, 2021.

Sigrist, Christian; Regulierte Anarchie, 1967.

Sinn, Hans-Werner; Der Mythos vom Marshall-Plan, 03.02.2023.
https://www.hanswernersinn.de/de/marshallp lan-brackmann-hb-03022023

Sinn, Hans-Werner;
https://www.hanswernersinn.de/de.

SIPRI – Stockholm International Peace Research Institute. SIPRI: https://www.sipri.org/databases/armstransfers.

Smith, Adam; Der Wohlstand der Nationen, Erstveröffentlichung 1776.

Spangler, David; The Flame of Incarnation, First edition, 2009.

Spengler, Oswald; Der Untergang des Abendlandes, erster Band 1918, zweiter Band 1922.
Spethmann, Dieter; Deutschland verschenkt seinen Wohlstand, am 19.01.2011 in der FAZ.

Spykman, Nicholas J.; Geography and Foreign Policy", published in The American Political Science Review, Vol. XXXII, Nos. 1 and 2, February and April 1938.

Steinbuch, Karl; Falsch programmiert – Über das Versagen unserer Gesellschaft in der Gegenwart und vor der Zukunft, 1968.

Steiner, Rudolf; Band GA 335 der Gesamtausgabe.

Steiner, Rudolf; Gesamtausgabe Band GA 185, Vorträge von 1918.

Stephanson, Anders; Manifest Destiny: American Expansionism and the Empire of Right, 1995.

Straubhaar, Thomas; Der Untergang ist abgesagt: Wider die Mythen des Demographischen Wandels, 2016.

Thomas, Anthony; Rhodes: the Race for Africa, 1997.

Tiger, Lionel und Fox, Robin; The Imperial Animal, 1976.

Todd, Emmanuel; La Défaite de l'Occident, von 2024.

Todd, Emmanuel; Weltmacht USA: ein Nachruf, 2003.

Tofler, Alvin ; Revolutionary Wealth, 2006.

Toynbee, Arnold J.; Essay aus dem Jahre 1934. "Things Not Foreseen at Paris; The Future in Retrospect".

Vidal, Gore; Perpetual War for Perpetual Peace: How we got to be so hated. American Imperialism, Book 1", 2002.

Wallerstein, Immanuel; Aufstieg und zukünftiger Niedergang des kapitalistischen Weltsystems. Zur Grundlegung vergleichender Analyse. In: Senghaas, Dieter (Hrsg.): Kapitalistische Weltökonomie. Kontroversen über ihren Ursprung und ihre Entwicklungsdynamik, 1979 und 1982.

Wallerstein, Immanuel; The Capitalist World-Economy, 1979.

Wang, Mingyuan; Why Have Repeated Efforts to Revitalize the Northeast Failed? – Rethinking the Twentieth Anniversary of the Strategy of Revitalizing the Old Industrial base.
https://www.readingthechinadream.com/wang-mingyuan-on-chinas-northeast.html.

Warburg, Paul M.; The Federal Reserve System: its origin and growth; reflections and recollections; 2 volumes, New York 1930.

Weidenhausen, Gerd; Buchbesprechung, in Die Drei, Nr. 5.: Wolfgang Bittner, Die Eroberung Europas durch die USA, 2015.

Wendt, Reinhard; Vom Kolonialismus zur Globalisierung: Europa und die Welt seit 1500, 2016.

Wiener, Norbert; The Human Use of Human Beings – Cybernetics and Society, 1950.

Wilhelm, Richard; Die Seele Chinas, 1925.

Willke, Hellmut; Global Governance, 2006.

Willke, Helmut; Atopia, 2001.

Wulf, Andrea; Alexander von Humboldt und die Erfindung der Natur, deutsch 2016.

Wüthrich, Werner; Europäische Integration, in dem Schweizer Magazin «Zeit-Fragen» von 2011 bis 2012.

Zeit-Fragen, Nr. 38, 2010: Studie zur „Geschichte der EU – Teil 1.

Zhao, Tingyang; Alles unter einem Himmel - Vergangenheit und Zukunft der Weltordnung, 2019.

ZHAO, Tingyang; All under Heaven: The Tianxia System for a Possible World Order, 2016.

Zürcher Kantonalbank, CBO, Census, OMB. https://www.zkb.ch/de/blog/anlegen/us-staatsverschuldung-rekordkurs.html.

Zürn, Michael; A Theory of Global Governance: Authority, Legitimacy and Contestation, 2018.